Southeastern

THE GIANT PANDA

Look for these and other books in the
Lucent Endangered Animals and Habitats series:

The Elephant
The Giant Panda
The Oceans
The Rhinoceros
The Shark
The Whale

Other related titles in the Lucent Overview series:

Acid Rain
Endangered Species
Energy Alternatives
Garbage
The Greenhouse Effect
Ocean Pollution
Oil Spills
Ozone
Pesticides
Population
Rainforests
Recycling
Vanishing Wetlands
Zoos

Introduction

THE GIANT PANDA is one of the world's rarest animals. Playful, friendly, and childlike, the panda appeals to people of all ages, who respond to news of panda pregnancies, births, or deaths anywhere in the world with phone calls, greeting cards, and public prayers.

Very proud that these beautiful animals are found only in their country, the Chinese people have accorded the giant panda the status of "national treasure" and adopted it as a symbol of China, in the same way that the bald eagle is a national symbol of the United States. However, like the bald eagle, the giant panda's population in the wild is dwindling. The giant panda is among the most critically endangered species in the world. The first scientific census of giant pandas, taken between 1974 and 1977, indicated the existence of about eleven hundred wild pandas. By 1986 this number had dropped to seven hundred. The exact number is unknown because even field biologists find giant pandas difficult to locate in their natural habitat.

Causes for endangerment

Ten thousand years ago, the giant panda's domain stretched through Laos, Burma, Vietnam, and China. Two factors caused the giant panda to vanish from these regions: First, a gradual, irreversible change to a drier climate in these areas eliminated its major food source, bamboo, which grows best in damp areas. The second factor, which occurred in the past century, was an exponential increase in China's human population. China is only

Contents

THE GIANT PANDA

BY JUDITH JANDA PRESNALL

Endangered Animals & Habitats

LUCENT BOOKS, INC.
SAN DIEGO, CALIFORNIA

To my daughter, Kaye Lynn

Library of Congress Cataloging-in-Publication Data

Presnall, Judith Janda
    The Giant Panda / by Judith Janda Presnall.
      p.   cm. — (Endangered animals & habitats)
    Includes bibliographical references (p.   ) and index.
    Summary: Discusses the forces pushing the giant panda toward
extinction and the efforts being made to counter those forces.
    ISBN 1-56006-463-3 (alk. paper)
    1. Giant panda—Juvenile literature. 2. Endangered species—
Juvenile literature.   [1. Giant panda. 2. Pandas. 3. Endangered
species.]   I. Title. II. Series.
QL737.C214P74   1998
599.789—dc21
                                           97-27276
                                              CIP
                                              AC

Copyright © 1998 by Lucent Books, Inc.
P.O. Box 289011, San Diego, CA 92198-9011
Printed in the U.S.A.

The giant panda, one of the world's most beloved animals, is also one of the most threatened as a species.

roughly 5 percent greater than the United States in area, but has four times the population. In need of more living space, people cleared the mountain foothills for farms, rice paddies, and settlements large and small. As its bamboo was chopped down, the giant panda moved higher into the mountains.

Today, giant pandas are found in only a few remote mountain regions in central China. Hemmed in by human development and cultivated land, they have no place else to go. Habitat loss, genetic isolation of wild panda populations, poaching, and the cyclical dying off of bamboo forests threaten the pandas with extinction.

Aid from humans

Human intervention may be the panda's only hope for survival. Some limited success has been achieved with natural and artificial breeding programs. Other human efforts include control of forest development, building panda "corridors" to link isolated panda populations, and imposing stiff jail terms on poachers. But if these human measures do not have an appreciable and immediate effect, the black-and-white creatures may soon be found only as stuffed toys on store shelves.

Chinese and American field biologists have undertaken collaborative studies of pandas in the bamboo forests in hopes that their research will lead not only to a better understanding of the species, but also to possible ways the Chinese government can preserve the animal's only true habitat. Panda expert George B. Schaller says, "It's easy to save the panda. All it needs is bamboo and peace."

But what sacrifices must be made to save the giant panda? Can enough land be set aside for pandas in protective reserves? Is it worth the cost to relocate residents who live in panda areas? Will even successful captive breeding projects translate into panda population growth in the wild? Will the international community aid China financially and scientifically in its efforts to save the panda? What has been done so far to protect the giant panda? What more can be done to ensure its survival? And, fundamentally, is human intervention called for? Competing interests have little time to debate and decide these issues.

1

The Giant Panda: A Profile

VIRTUALLY EVERYONE WHO has seen a living giant panda has visited a zoo exhibit. Fewer than fifty westerners have seen a giant panda in the wild. In their remote habitat of dense bamboo forests, the tree-sitting animals are difficult even for experts to track. But although the panda's life in the wild remains largely mysterious, much can be surmised by studying captive giant pandas.

Ancestry

The Chinese traditionally thought the giant panda was a kind of bear. They had many names for it—the clawed bear, the bamboo bear, the harlequin bear, the speckled bear, the cat-bear—but most often they called it *bei-shung*, the white bear. The giant panda looks and walks like a bear. Its newborn cubs are very tiny, like a bear's. A panda climbs trees like a bear. Laboratory analysis shows the animal even has bearlike blood.

A missionary priest, Père Armand David, who was also a naturalist, announced the discovery of the panda to the West in 1869, and gave it the scientific name of *Ursus melanoleucus*, which meant "black and white bear." However, when he sent a panda's skeleton and hide to Professor Alphonse Milne-Edwards at a natural history museum in Paris, the professor did not think it was a bear. The skull was not like a bear's. This skull had a shorter muzzle and was heavier and more solid. The jaws and teeth were also

Each front paw of the giant panda has a padded thumblike appendage used to grasp and hold objects.

unlike a bear's, as were the skeleton's feet and legs. Milne-Edwards changed the creature's taxonomic name to *Ailuropoda melanoleucus,* meaning "black and white cat-foot."

Zoologists also noted that the five-toed panda had a peculiar extra appendage on its front paws that worked like a human thumb. No bear has a sixth digit. However, one other animal also has a modified wristbone that acts as an opposable thumb. That raccoon-like animal, called the red panda, also grips and eats bamboo leaves and shoots. The twelve-pound red panda has a red coat, white face, and a bushy ringed tail. It, too, lives in the mountains of China and, like a panda, climbs trees. The skull, grinding teeth, and foot bones are similar to those of the giant panda. The stomach, liver, and intestines of the giant panda are more like that of a raccoon than that of a bear.

Bear family or racoon family

Giant pandas have the same number of chromosomes in their cells as raccoons—forty-two. (Bears have seventy-four chromosomes.) Unlike bears, giant pandas do not hibernate. Except for the color of its coat and long tail, the red panda resembles a small version of the giant panda.

As noted, giant pandas share characteristics with both bears and raccoons. Consequently, zoologists have argued for more than a century over the ancestry of the giant panda; taxonomists could not agree on its proper classification.

In the November 1987 issue of *Scientific American*, author Stephen J. O'Brien discusses the conclusions reached by several scientists in trying to solve the riddle of the panda's ancestry:

As recently as 1964 D. Dwight Davis, curator of mammals at the Field Museum of Natural History in Chicago, published an extensive account of the anatomy of the *Ailuropoda* and concluded on the basis of 50 organ systems that the panda was a member of the bear family. Soon thereafter Desmond Morris, curator at the Zoological Society of London, and R. F. Ewer of the University of Ghana independently concluded on behavioral and morphological [form and structure] grounds that the giant panda belonged in the raccoon family.

Some scientists disagreed with both arguments. They did not think the giant panda belonged in either the bear or the raccoon family. They believed it belonged in a family of its own—the panda family.

Molecular biology solves the riddle

In the late 1980s, scientists used advances in molecular biology to determine that giant pandas are a subfamily of bears. DNA (hereditary material) from the giant panda, the red panda, the raccoon, and several bear species was compared. Each of the giant panda's forty-two chromosomes was discovered to have been a fused or head-to-head pair. If cut in half, the new total was closer to the seventy-four count of bear chromosomes. Based on many such chromosome tests, scientists made the taxonomic (classification) recommendation that the giant panda belongs in the bear family with its own subfamily name.

The raccoonlike red panda (pictured here) and the giant panda share the same diet and territory.

Experts in the study of animal behavior are called "ethologists." *Scientific American* reported a recommendation by ethologists John F. Eisenberg of the University of Florida and George B. Schaller of the New York Zoological Society

> that the giant panda be placed in its own family, the *Ailuropodidae*. That view was endorsed in 1986 by a team of Chinese scientists including several from the Beijing Zoo and Beijing University, who published a lengthy anatomical account of the panda.

Thus, the riddle of panda ancestry has been solved. Based on the molecular biology analysis, the giant panda was found to be more closely related to bears than to raccoons. And therefore, the giant panda is classified as a subfamily of bears. However, because it is sufficiently different from bears, it has its own classification, *Ailuropoda melanoleuca*. The red panda was found to be more closely related to the raccoon, and it, too, has been classified in its own subfamily, *Ailurus fulgens.*

Giant panda characteristics

The tubby, bearlike animal has distinctive black features against a thick, woolly white coat. Although panda fur looks soft, it is actually stiff and coarse. Its coarse, waterproof coat protects it from the cold in its damp, misty habitat. Its contrasting black features include eye patches; small, erect, rounded ears; short legs; and shoulder bands.

The giant panda's black and white fur serves as a camouflage when viewed against tree branches and the sky.

The coloring is actually an effective camouflage. At the first sign of danger, the panda climbs a tree and squats on a forked branch. There, its black markings blend with trunks, branches, and shadows. Its white parts are almost invisible against the bright sky.

In his book *Pandas*, Chris Catton recounts a legend that Chinese mothers tell their children explaining how the panda acquired its black markings:

A young and beautiful girl lived in the Wolong valley with her family. She was a shepherdess, loved by all who knew her for her kindness and good nature. Whenever she took her sheep into the hills a young panda would come to join her flock, perhaps mistaking them for its own kind for in those days pandas were all white.

One day the panda arrived as usual, but it had not been playing with the flock for long when a leopard jumped from a tree and began to savage [attack] the helpless cub. Careless of her own life, the girl picked up a stick and began to beat the leopard. The panda ran off, but the leopard turned on its attacker and killed her.

When the other pandas heard this, they were stricken with grief. All came to attend the girl's funeral, and as a mark of their respect they covered their arms with ashes as was the custom. At the funeral, they could not contain themselves. They wiped their eyes to dry their tears, and hugged themselves as they sobbed. The cries became so loud that they covered their ears with their paws to block out the noise. Wherever they touched themselves the ashes stained their fur black and since that day all pandas have carried these marks.

In less romantic terms, giant pandas grow as large as American black bears, which is four to six feet from nose to stubby tail. In comparison, grizzly bears grow to be about seven feet in length and polar bears as long as eleven feet. Giant pandas are not really giants in the sense that an elephant is a giant. One average elephant weighs more than thirty giant pandas.

Distinctive traits

The giant panda is so named in order to differentiate it from the small red panda, which is also endangered. Sometimes called the lesser panda, the forty-four-inch-long (including its nineteen-inch tail) red panda looks like a raccoon. Because their ranges overlap and both the giant and lesser panda depend on a bamboo diet, they are both threatened by the same human and ecological pressures.

In the wild, female giant pandas weigh about 200 pounds and males weigh up to 240 pounds. But in a zoo, giant pandas grow much heavier because their routines are sedentary; that is, in zoos they do not use energy foraging for food or searching for a mate. A male panda in the Moscow Zoo, Ping-Ping, weighed 399 pounds. And at the Bronx Zoo in New York, a female panda named Panduh weighed 379 pounds.

The panda's short, shaggy tail is concealed in its hindquarters and is barely visible. The tail protects the panda's scent glands and is used to "paint" the animal's scent wherever it wants to mark its territory or send a message to other pandas.

Although adult giant pandas have few natural enemies, the young are sometimes preyed upon by leopards, Asiatic wild dogs, and brown bears. Predators of the giant panda also include humans who kill the panda for its pelt. Though generally characterized as a shy, passive animal, if the panda feels threatened by humans in the wild, it will aggressively charge them. During field studies, pandas have been known to enter huts and tents in search of food, quickly clearing out any people who may have been occupying the tent at the time.

Reported in *The Giant Panda*, George B. Schaller followed a male panda, Wei-Wei, for five-and-a-half days, keeping detailed notes about his activities: "[Wei-Wei] averaged just over three-quarters of a mile of travel a day . . . left his scent on forty-five trees, . . . had nine lengthy rest periods, . . . and deposited an average of ninety-seven droppings per day." On another day reserved just for calculating how much bamboo Wei-Wei consumed, Schaller recorded: "Wei-Wei had consumed parts of about twenty-two hundred stems and a portion of the leaves from nearly fourteen hundred stems, or about thirty-one pounds of bamboo."

The panda's eye patches enlarge the appearance of its small, dark eyes tenfold, allowing them to present a threatening stare to a foe. However, pandas have poor eyesight, which is one reason they are unable to hunt prey successfully.

On each foot, the panda has five toes equipped with sharp claws, useful for climbing trees, digging, and defending itself. Only on its front paws are the panda's five fingers supported by its padded "thumb," useful for holding food and other objects.

Diet

Bamboo plants provide 99 percent of the wild giant panda's diet. Bamboo is really a family of grasses with woody stems roughly one-and-a-half inches thick that can grow as tall as trees. Pandas eat the stems, twigs, leaves, branches, and fresh young shoots of the bamboo. Wild pandas also eat flowering plants such as irises and crocuses. Although the panda is not usually a successful hunter, it is, like bears, a carnivore, and will occasionally eat fish and small rodents such as voles and pikas.

Everywhere a panda goes in a bamboo forest, it is surrounded by food. Sitting on its rump, it grabs a bamboo stalk with its front paw, pulls it down, and uses its strong teeth not only to snap or bite it off, but also to strip off the tough outer covering to get to the softer pith inside. The panda's powerful jawbones work with huge cheek muscles to crush the fibrous stalk. Using broad, flat molars, it can crunch a whole stalk in about forty seconds and may chew on more than 650 stems a day. Pandas prefer tender bamboo shoots and leaves when they can get them. Sometimes

Bamboo is the staple of a giant panda's diet.

a panda will clip off leaf after leaf until a large bouquet has accumulated in the corner of its mouth and then go to work on the bunch a mouthful at a time. Scientists calculate a panda's bamboo intake to be about 66 pounds a day, or 25,000 pounds of food each year.

Pandas eat large quantities because their intestines are too short to digest plant food properly, that is, thoroughly. They have the digestive system of a carnivorous, or meat-eating, animal; but a few million years ago, their ancestors, finding meat scarce, gradually replaced their meat diet with bamboo, which was plentiful. However, though the panda diet gradually became vegetarian, its intestines remained short. Because the panda has a short gut, much of the bamboo that quickly passes through it remains undigested. Thus, in order to get enough nourishment to stay alive, the panda must eat often.

The panda's intestines are about thirty-three feet long. In comparison, a cow, which is vegetarian, or herbivorous, has a much longer gut—130 to 164 feet long—and its contents take longer to pass through the intestines. The disadvantage of eating the low-nutrition bamboo is that the panda has to spend a great deal of its time satisfying its hunger. It is fortunate for pandas that bamboo grows year-round and that few other animals compete for this food.

There are over twelve hundred species of bamboo throughout the world, about three hundred of which are native to China. Somewhat choosy, pandas will eat about twenty of these. Although pandas generally drink from mountain streams and rivulets, they get most of their moisture from bamboo, which is 90 percent water. Ten to sixteen hours of a panda's day are spent just on nourishing its body. The remainder of the time pandas wander, search for food, rest, and sleep.

Lifestyle and activities

The giant panda is a solitary animal. Each panda has its own territory, or range, which is about one-and-a-half to four square miles. Normally, it will spend its entire life in that one area. Occasionally ranges overlap: The panda does

not mind if another panda moves into its range, as long as it does not come too close.

The giant panda walks in slow, long, pigeon-toed steps, its large head swaying from side to side. The panda's muscular upper body is very strong. (Pandas in zoos destroy their toys very quickly.) However, the rear legs are comparatively weak. This may be one reason why pandas don't seem to run very fast. Even when pandas are being chased, they move in a slow trot.

A wild panda cleans its fur by rolling in dry dirt, combing the dirt from its fur with its claws, and licking itself clean. The giant panda also uses its sharp claws to pull itself up into trees, where it perches for hours or overnight.

In *Pandas*, Miriam Schlein describes the panda's daily routine:

> Day and night, pandas keep wandering and eating. When they get tired, they rest wherever they happen to be. They lean against a tree or lie down in the snow, and sleep a while. Usually they sleep from two to four hours, but sometimes for just a few minutes. Their thick oily fur keeps them warm and dry. Winter and summer, their routine is more or less the same.

The panda's sluggish gait reflects its relaxed attitude.

Because pandas are surrounded by food, they do not travel very far in a day—maybe six hundred feet, which is about two short city blocks. They seek each other out only in the spring, during the breeding season.

Pandas conserve energy by economizing their activities. For example, they travel over moderate terrain rather than up and down steep slopes. Males remain in small ranges and do not defend territorial boundaries. Females use little energy in reproduction. Both communicate by scent, thus avoiding direct social interaction.

Finding a mate

Pandas have a good sense of smell. Rubbing their rumps against a tree trunk, stump, or rock, they leave a sticky message to other pandas. Called "scent-marking," the behavior is typical year-round.

Scent-marking leaves valuable information: whether the panda is male or female, whether it is in rut (ready to mate), and how long ago it was there. During spring breeding season, the forest becomes noisy with pandas barking, snorting, mooing, bleating, chirping, and yipping songs for mates.

Giant pandas reach breeding maturity anywhere from age four to ten years. (Each year of age for a panda is equivalent to about three human years.) Female pandas are fertile only once a year for about twelve to twenty-five days, between mid-March and mid-May. However, the peak receptivity (desire) to mate lasts only two to five days.

Males compulsively follow a female's scent marks. But the female does not submit to the male until she has become accustomed to him. She may climb a tree, swat him, or bite his nose if she is not ready to mate. During the panda's ovulation period, she may have two to five males competing for her and mating with her.

In *The Giant Panda*, Jin Xuqi describes a male panda's search for a mate:

> The male may have to wait a long time before the female accepts him. He sometimes shows his feelings by climbing a tree and giving a series of muffled barks and roars. At the same time he tries to impress the female with what a bold and

resourceful creature he really is. His roars are intended partly for that purpose and partly to warn off other males who may be inclined to appear and perhaps disrupt the mating. It may be several days before the female is willing to accept the male. His patience is eventually rewarded and he is allowed to approach and mate with her.

After mating, pandas go their separate ways. The male has no role in caring for offspring.

Birth and growing up

Baby pandas are born in late summer or early autumn following a four- to five-month gestation. The mother panda gives birth in a protected place, such as a cave, under a ledge, or in a large (three-foot diameter) hollow fir tree, which she has lined with bamboo twigs. Though she typically gives birth to a litter of two hamster-sized cubs, usually the mother will focus on only one cub and let the other die, probably because her capacity is limited: The mother cradles her cub in a front paw or carries it in her

A mother panda nuzzles her cub. The cub will remain with her until it reaches the age of eighteen months.

mouth wherever she goes. There have been exceptions to raising only one cub, however. In 1990, twins about three weeks old were discovered in a cave in Wolong in the Sichuan Province in central China. Also that year, a female at the Chengdu Zoo in Sichuan raised twins.

The surviving cub weighs three to five ounces, 1/800th the size of its mother. Distinctive black-and-white markings (skin pigmentation) show through its baby fuzz. The newborn has a loud cry; if left alone, its cry may attract predators such as leopards and wild dogs. Thus, for the first few weeks the conscientious mother never lets go of the cub. Cuddling, nursing, and licking it, she is a devoted parent.

In a February 1993 issue of *National Geographic*, author Lü Zhi shares her firsthand observation of the birth of a panda cub. In the southern Shaanxi Province, she and Professor Pan Wenshi tracked a radio-collared pregnant panda, Jiao Jiao:

> I heard a delicate sound, between a puppy's whimper and a foal's whinny. . . . The cub, pink and fragile, wriggled up [its] mother's chest and disappeared behind a sheltering paw. We made some [other] discoveries: We learned that, like true bears, panda mothers sometimes fast after giving birth. We saw Jiao Jiao stay with Xi Wang [the newborn cub] continuously, not feeding or defecating for 25 days. . . . More important, perhaps, Jiao Jiao consumes all the infant's wastes— whose smell could attract predators, such as the lethal minklike yellow-throated marten.

At one month, black-and-white fur covers the cub's body and it looks clearly like a panda. The cub's eyes open at about six weeks. When it begins to crawl, the mother carries the cub in one front paw and walks on three legs.

Panda cubs grow rapidly

At ten weeks, the baby panda begins taking steps. Mother pandas cuddle their cubs often and allow the cubs to climb all over their bodies. At the age of three months, the cub weighs about twelve pounds and is two feet long. When the cub is five months old, it will trot beside its mother. The mother feeds milk to her cub as much as four-

teen hours a day until it is nine to twelve months old. Having about twenty-eight teeth at six months of age, the cub can begin eating some bamboo. However, it does not adopt its regular diet of bamboo until around the age of one year.

A panda cub uses its mother for a mattress as it naps.

The young cub will stay with its mother for about eighteen months. By then it weighs over one hundred pounds and is ready to settle into its own range. Because a female panda takes eighteen months to raise her offspring, she reproduces only once every two years.

In *National Geographic*, Lü Zhi and her partner also report another observance made during their three years in the Qin Ling Mountains:

> We found that Jiao Jiao and Hu Zi [Jiao Jiao's firstborn cub] stayed together two and a half years, about a year longer than most researchers thought was the norm. Jiao Jiao finally chased her son off in March 1992, after she came into heat and mated with Xi Wang's father.

In the best of circumstances, a female panda will raise four or five cubs during her lifetime. But faced with limited feeding areas, attacks by poachers, and other threats,

only two cubs out of a possible five are likely to survive to adulthood. In zoos, giant pandas may live to be over thirty years old; their life span is unknown in the wild, but is thought to be less than twenty years.

Habitat

The only place in the world where giant pandas live is in the dense bamboo and coniferous forests of central China, at altitudes of 5,000 to 12,000 feet. Their range comprises specific areas of three provinces situated far from population centers. These small isolated tracts include the north and central mountains of Sichuan Province, the mountains bordering the southern part of Gansu Province, and the Qin Ling Mountains of Shaanxi Province.

Shrouded in heavy clouds, the mountainous forests are misty throughout the year. Panda country has snow in the winter and rain in the summer. More than fifty inches of rain and snow may fall every year, an ideal climate for the water-loving bamboo.

Lush bamboo grows to be over seven feet tall in this area. Because the forest is so dense, giant pandas are difficult to spot. In *Pandas*, Chris Catton describes the land and the growth of bamboo at various altitudes:

> Although the terrain is difficult with many mountains over 4,500 m [15,000 feet], steep slopes, and deep valleys, the vegetation is not as unremittingly impenetrable . . . . Around 3,400 m [11,000 feet] the forest is actually quite open with

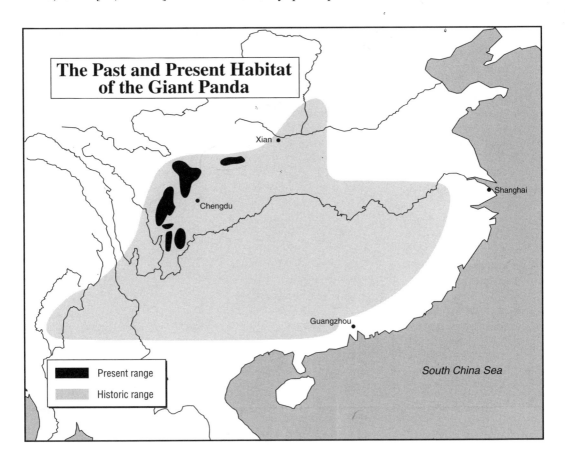

only a relatively sparse covering of bamboo beneath the dense canopy of firs. The bamboos that grow at these altitudes are generally slender plants, with stems rarely more than a metre [39.37 inches] tall and no thicker than a pencil. Lower down . . . the forest is denser. Taller bamboo species, like the umbrella bamboo grows to a height of 2.5–3 m [8 to 10 feet]. This bamboo really is unpleasant to move through, since the tangled live stems must constantly be pushed aside. . . . Below about 2,000 m [6,500 feet] the character of the forest changes again. . . . A wider variety of bamboos grow in this forest and bamboo thickets are difficult to move through, but once again, large tracts of forest have only a sparse under-storey.

At one time, the mountainous region was inaccessible to most travelers. Now, however, roads have been cut into the area that allow access to the giant pandas' habitat but make their future in the wild even more uncertain.

Once the giant panda was discovered, its rarity and exotic beauty spurred game hunters' desire to capture it as a trophy—a prize to bring back to parts of the world beyond China, dead or alive.

2

Pandas Wanted: Dead and Alive!

IN THE SECOND century B.C., the Chinese regarded the giant panda as a semidivine and rare animal. During the Han dynasty (206 B.C.–A.D. 24), the emperor's garden held nearly forty rare species of animals. The most treasured of these was the panda. Poet Bai Juyi, who lived from A.D. 772 to 846, credited the panda with the power to prevent disease and exorcise evil spirits.

Throughout Chinese history, panda skins were presented as gifts or tributes on state occasions. However, for centuries the panda's existence was kept a secret within the Chinese Empire. But near the end of the nineteenth century, when China opened its borders to trade and to Christianity, the panda could no longer be kept a secret.

Wildlife discoveries by missionary Père Armand David

Christian missionaries played a key role in alerting the West about Chinese wildlife. Protestant and Catholic missionaries from the United States and Europe collected plants and animals and sent them back to their native lands. One Vincentian missionary priest, Père (Father) Armand David, was assigned to teach science to boys at a small school in Beijing. Père David was well-known for his knowledge of flora and fauna. Consequently, in addition to his teaching assignment, the director of France's Muséum d'Histoire Naturelle, Henri Milne-Edwards, asked Père David to collect specimens of any interesting plants and animals.

Soon Père David's missionary work took a secondary role to his collecting. In 1866, impressed with the specimens that Père David sent back to France, Milne-Edwards persuaded the superior-general of the Lazarist order to send Père David to other areas of China where he could collect more wildlife.

One specimen-rich collecting area was southeastern China. In one four-month period in Kiangsi, Père David sent collections to the museum of around 30 species of birds, 10 species of mammals, 60 species of reptiles and fish, over 630 species of insects, and 200 species of plants.

Hunting the panda for science

Upon returning from an excursion one day, Père David and his hunters were invited to rest and have tea at the home of the Muping Valley's (now Baoxing) principal landowner. This landowner was a hunter, and it was at his home that Père David first saw a giant panda skin. In *Abbe David's Diary* (translated from French by Helen M. Fox), for March 11, 1869, the following is recorded:

> At this pagan's [house] I see a fine skin of the famous white and black bear, which appears to be fairly large. It is a remarkable species and I am delighted when I hear my hunters say that I shall certainly obtain the animal within a short time. They tell me, they will go out tomorrow to kill this animal, which will provide an interesting novelty for science.

According to Père David's diary entry for March 23:

> My Christian hunters return today after a ten-day absence. They bring me a young white bear, which they took alive but unfortunately killed so it could be carried more easily. The young white bear, which they sell to me very dearly [at a high price], is all white except for the legs, ears, and around the eyes, which are deep black. The colors are the same as those I saw in the skin of an adult bear the other day at the home of Li, the hunter. This must be a new species of *Ursus* [bear], very remarkable not only because of its color, but also for its paws, which are hairy underneath, and for other characters.

Later, from his room at the Catholic College of Muping in the Min Mountains, Père David wrote a letter to Alphonse Milne-Edwards, Henri's son, listing his recent acquisitions. In the letter Père David also gave a brief description of his latest find, the giant panda.

A week later, Père David's hunters brought him the carcass of an adult female giant panda. Several days later he had two red panda specimens. Because Père David had limited resources to do detailed anatomical work, he shipped the carcasses of both the giant panda and red panda to Alphonse Milne-Edwards in Paris. Thus, Milne-Edwards had an opportunity to dissect them and was given the honor of assigning a scientific name to the giant panda.

As it turned out, Père David never saw a live giant panda in the wild, only the carcasses. On his final journey to

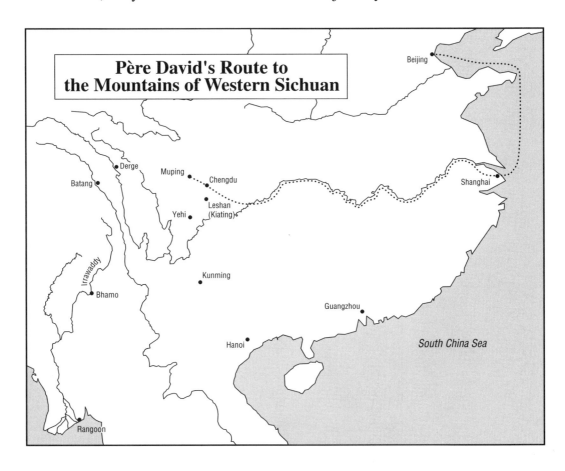

Père David's Route to the Mountains of Western Sichuan

Shaanxi and Gansu Provinces, he spent three months collecting other specimens in the Qin Ling Mountains. This area was home to a large population of giant pandas, but Père David never mentioned them in his journals of this trip.

Little was heard of the giant panda for a half a century after that. Possibly no westerner set eyes on a live panda until 1914, when German zoologist Hugo Weigold was presented with a live cub by local hunters. The cub was still a suckling, and since Weigold could not provide it with suitable food, it soon died. The cub's hide, along with five others purchased from hunters, eventually went on display in the Berlin Museum.

Doomed as a prized trophy

In the 1920s, incomplete maps of the Tibetan plateau encouraged adventurous people to explore the area. Western big game hunters relished the idea of being the first to stalk

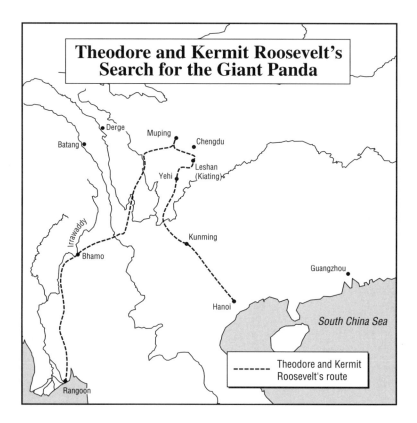

animals in new frontiers. To shoot a giant panda became the supreme goal. The first hunters from the United States were the sons of Theodore Roosevelt, American president from 1901 to 1909.

Kermit and Theodore Jr. had inherited a yearning for adventure from their father. Irresistibly drawn to the rugged Himalayas, the brothers looked forward to traveling through uncharted country. Kermit and Theodore were so intent on their goal of shooting a panda that they had no fears, only optimism. In their book *Trailing the Giant Panda*, Theodore explains:

> The Golden Fleece of our trip was the giant panda. *Aeluropus melanoleucus* is its scientific name. It lives in the dense bamboo jungles in Szechuan, and authorities seemed to agree that so far it had never been killed by a white man.

The Roosevelts used their political connections to obtain the Chinese government's permission to enter the borderlands. They invited other adventurous men to join them, and ultimately their group included a British scientist, a trained naturalist, a doctor, and a professor.

Searching for the elusive panda

Leaving New York in November 1928, the Roosevelt brothers and their entourage traveled by ship, train, and river steamer to reach the Burmese city Bhamo by Christmas Eve. It took another three months of hard walking with a team of thirty pack mules to travel from Burma into China. They trudged through the mountains of Yunnan and Sichuan before finally arriving in Muping.

Accompanied by fourteen native hunters, Kermit and Theodore searched for six days without seeing any wild animals. In anticipation of sighting a panda, Theodore Roosevelt describes in *Trailing the Giant Panda* an agreement he had made with his brother Kermit:

> We both felt that if we saw a panda it would be but once. We therefore decided that if we were together we should give up our old custom of matching for the first shot, and fire if possible simultaneously. We wanted to be full partners in the first panda, should the gods permit.

In this 1932 photo at Chicago's Field Museum of Natural History, Theodore Roosevelt Jr. (left) stands next to a display of giant pandas. He had killed the pandas while on a hunting expedition and later donated them to the museum.

On April 13, 1929, the group, along with hired Muping hunters, followed a snowy trail for over two hours before they came to an open jungle. Finding a bamboo nest, claw marks, and giant panda tracks, the stalkers knew they were close to finding their trophy. With their hearts racing, they watched as a large sleepy panda emerged from the hollowed trunk of a giant spruce.

"As soon as Ted came up," Kermit said, "we fired simultaneously at the outline of the disappearing panda." The old male panda that the brothers shot was the first recorded killing of a panda in this Yehli region.

The Roosevelts' panda shooting set off a mass of Western hunting expeditions. Museums sponsored these expeditions because they were eager to secure a giant panda specimen for exhibition. In 1931, the Philadelphia Academy of Natural Sciences sent a large expedition to China that netted them a total of four slain adult panda specimens. For the next few years, panda skins and carcasses were bought from local hunters and sent to the United States by missionaries. Museums were eager for stuffed panda specimens to grace their exhibition halls for curious Americans. Because of the panda's extensive range and elusiveness, there are no recorded panda population figures for this period. The panda has always been a rare species sparsely distributed. The next challenge would be to capture a live giant panda for a Western zoo.

Capturing the giant panda

The first documented response to the challenge of capturing a panda came from Americans: William Harvest Harkness Jr., his bride, Ruth, and Floyd Tangier Smith.

William Harkness Jr. was a Harvard graduate with a craving for exotic travel and adventure. Harkness had already supplied the Bronx Zoo in New York with several Komodo dragons from what was then the Dutch East Indies. Now he set out to obtain a giant panda for the zoo. Harkness left New York on September 22, 1934, with his five-man expedition. Ruth Harkness reluctantly remained in New York.

When Harkness arrived in China in January 1935, he encountered difficulty in getting formal permits for his expedition. It would be thirteen months before the Academia Sinica in Nanking approved his credentials for the expedition. During this long delay, he met Floyd Tangier Smith, a veteran hunter in China.

Tangier Smith, born in 1882 to wealthy American parents, was educated in the United States and Japan and eventually settled in Shanghai, where he devoted his time to daring outdoor pursuits. Smith collected and sold rare flora and fauna; he acquired an international reputation for the quantity and quality of his animal captures for Asian and Western zoos and museums. Although Smith had hunted in China for nearly twenty years, he had never so much as caught a glimpse of a live giant panda. His ultimate goal was to capture one and take it to the United States. Harkness and Smith joined forces in an elaborate scheme to achieve their common goal.

But Harkness never fulfilled his dream of capturing a giant panda. Political turmoil and civil war in China derailed his plan. During the joint expedition, the Nationalist government of Chiang Kai-shek would not allow representatives from foreign countries to enter the unstable region, so the two hunters had to turn back. By the time the ban was lifted, Harkness had taken sick and died in a Shanghai hospital.

Harkness's wife, Ruth, grew up in Titusville, Pennsylvania. But she radiated the sophistication of a suave Manhattan socialite. She also was determined enough to accomplish whatever she set her mind to. Two months after her husband's death, the tiny, elegant dress designer set out to continue her husband's work. Ruth wrote in her book *The Lady and the Panda*:

> In spite of what my friends and family had to say, I decided that it was up to me to do what I could in the way of carrying on. Everything was there in China for me to work with; it was an opportunity, an excuse for adventure that would probably never come again. I had wanted to go in the first place, so why not now?

Ruth looked forward to meeting Tangier Smith. In her book, Ruth referred to him as "Zoology" Jones, "a boy of 55 or 60." Since they both assumed that Ruth would replace her husband as a hunting partner, Smith shared with her the locations of his camps. However, he tried to discourage her by insisting that the giant panda was too elusive to catch. Smith suggested she start with less exotic game. Ruth could not be diverted, and felt Smith's attitude was condescending. When the two could not agree on financial terms, as well, they ended their association amicably, and Ruth proceeded with her own plans to take a giant panda home for the Bronx Zoo.

Ruth Harkness's adventure

Ruth hired an expedition leader who was a keen hunter, Quentin Young. The twenty-two-year-old spoke fluent English and Cantonese as well as the Sichuan dialect of Mandarin. On September 26, 1936, the two of them began their 1,500-mile boat trip up the Yangtze River to

Adventurer and explorer Ruth Harkness feeds Su Lin, the first live panda cub brought to the United States.

Chongqing, followed by a 300-mile overland trek—first by car to Chengdu and then on foot to Wenchuan, where they hired a guide. For six weeks they fought the dense bamboo jungle with its seemingly impenetrable walls. They climbed over rotting fallen trees, trudged among moss-draped giant living trees, and zigzagged along deep gullies cut by running water.

In early November, Young and Harkness and twenty-one others in their party set up trapping camps in Tsaopo near what is now the Wolong Reserve. After ten days the hunters were rewarded for their efforts. In her book, Harkness describes her excitement when she, Young, and the guide found a baby panda:

> Dimly through waving wet branches I saw him [Quentin Young] near a huge rotting tree. I stumbled on blindly

brushing the water from my face and eyes. Then I too stopped, frozen in my tracks. From the old dead tree came a baby's whimper. I must have been momentarily paralyzed, for I didn't move until Quentin came toward me and held out his arms. There in the palms of his two hands was a squirming baby *bei-shung*.

First live panda leaves China

The task of transporting a hungry baby panda from the forests of China to the United States proved formidable. Young and Harkness took turns mixing dried milk and feeding the demanding cub from a bottle. They lined a canvas carrying case with flannel shirts for a cradle, which often got soaked with urine. They made diapers from torn bath towels. A guide carried the cub in a handwoven green bamboo basket strapped to his back. Harkness named the baby Su Lin, which means "a little bit of something very cute." The hunters judged the three-pound cub to be about ten days old. The cub's eyes were still closed; its mother may have been frightened off by hunters' shots moments before the discovery.

Although Harkness experienced delays in leaving China with Su Lin, her expedition was successful. Su Lin, called a female, was exhibited in a Chicago zoo till its death sixteen months later. That panda and a captured mate (also by Harkness) were both determined to be males.

Eventually Tangier Smith was also successful in capturing his own live pandas. On Christmas Eve of 1938, he supplied the London Zoo with five pandas. The huge popularity of pandas was not a passing fad. The captures of the giant panda sent a message that was reiterated by Erika Brady in the December 1983 *Smithsonian*: "The heyday of the big-game hunter with his stuffed trophies was over. It was time, in the words of the famous animal collector Frank Buck, to 'bring 'em back alive.'"

Arthur de Carle Sowerby, who owned and edited a magazine titled *The China Journal* in the 1930s, published the following editorial about Su Lin's capture. His justification for relocating the animal reflects the general protectionist attitude of the day:

We cannot help admiring the action of the authorities, the Chinese Customs officials and others, who courageously gave the permit to take the Panda out of the country in the face of possible popular opinion that such a rare animal ought not to be allowed to leave China . . . for there can be no doubt whatever, that by getting the young Panda alive to a well-equipped institution for caring and rearing it to adulthood, the interests of science will best have been served. To have tried to keep it in China would undoubtedly have ended in disaster, and a great loss to scientific knowledge, for there is no institution in this country equipped to rear such a difficult animal to keep alive.

Poaching

But hunting to kill did not end in his era. According to George B. Schaller, director of Wildlife Conservation International, "The most serious [modern] problem by far is poaching." Young pandas are caught primarily for zoos, but adult pandas are still killed for their pelts. The panda's distinctive black-and-white skin is valued as rugs, sleeping mats, wall hangings, and coats. Hong Kong dealers and southern Chinese entrepreneurs dazzle farmers with offers of $2,000 to $4,000 for a panda skin. The main markets appear to be Japan, Hong Kong, and Taiwan, where one pelt can bring from $10,000 to $100,000 on the black market.

In October 1987, the Chinese Supreme Court warned that anyone found guilty of killing a giant panda or smuggling hides risked a jail sentence of between ten years to life in prison with the possibility of death. Apparently undeterred, however, poachers killed forty pandas in 1988. Eleven poachers were caught and given life sentences. In Schaller's *The Last Panda*, one poacher was quoted as saying to police in China's Public Security Newspaper: "I couldn't earn that much in a lifetime. Even though I risked my life, it was worth it. If you hadn't caught me, I would have been rich."

Panda meat itself is unpalatable, so little subsistence hunting occurs. Only the coveted panda pelt is sold on the black market. Because of the high prices paid for a skin, poachers have become unusually active and fearless. A 1989 article reports that Chinese officials have retrieved

150 panda skins from poachers in the past few years. The actual number of skins smuggled into Hong Kong is unknown. According to a 1994 *Los Angeles Times* article, the Chinese have reportedly executed six poachers, but the illegal traffic continues.

To control the problem of poaching, a 1992 Chinese management plan encourages rigorous patrolling, bringing poachers to trial, and closing down trade outlets for animal products. Patrolling efforts are funded by a variety of public and private organizations. These include the Chinese government's Ministry of Forestry, national nonprofit organizations, and the World Wildlife Fund. The perimeters of the preserves are patrolled for any illegal activities such as poaching, logging, and bamboo cutting. But the ultimate success of antipoaching programs is yet to be determined.

3

China's Mountains: The Panda's Threatened Habitat

UNLIKE HUNDREDS OF other large mammals that disappeared during climatic upheavals, the panda has endured. At one time the panda's domain stretched through Burma, Laos, Vietnam, and China. Today, however, pandas inhabit only six small regions deep in China's mountains, a tiny fraction of their former range. Humans have taken over most of the panda's habitat. With fewer than 1,000 giant pandas left in the world, their existence now depends primarily on the goodwill of humans.

Pandas can be found in three Chinese provinces: Sichuan (80 percent of the pandas live there in ten reserves), Gansu, and Shaanxi. This area is known as the "bamboo belt," a strip of bamboo forests 5,900 to 12,500 feet above sea level. The wildlife preserves cover an area of 2,500 square miles. Because the panda is confined to China, the greatest responsibility to preserve its natural habitat is left to that country. But, although China is the third largest country in the world (after the Russian Federation and Canada), it faces tremendous pressure to control its 1.2 billion population, the largest in the world. Despite such drastic and controversial policies as limiting families to one child, the demand for agricultural land, timbers, and other natural resources for human use remains great, and the panda's wilderness home continues to shrink.

Chinese people labor in rice paddies in Sichuan Province. The pandas' habitat is being reduced because of the great need for farmland in Chinese provinces.

People-related threats

The population in Sichuan Province in the 1930s was 50 million; by the 1980s the population had increased to 110 million. About 3,000 people inhabit the main valley in Sichuan's Wolong valley, a small area about one-eighth of the entire province. The good soil and mild climate permit up to three harvests per year. There, divided into two communes, inhabitants grow potatoes, maize (corn), beans, and other crops. Many mountainsides have been stripped below the level of 7,900 feet. The forest has either been cleared for fields and pastures or reduced to stunted vegetation, called scrub.

Cattle, sheep, and goats graze on emerging seedlings, which prevents regeneration of the forest. Also, their hooves loosen the thin mountain soil. Without tree cover, summer rains cause the soil to wash away, causing deep grooves and landslides. At an altitude of 13,000 feet, trees are slow to regrow. It may take eighty to ninety years for a tree trunk to grow eight to ten inches in diameter.

Agriculture

At low altitudes, the spread of agriculture has changed the bamboo areas into fields. Frequently, only one type of bamboo species grows in the higher ridges. When this species flowers and dies, pandas may be deprived of food until the bamboo regenerates.

Throughout the mid-1970s, the widespread starvation of pandas in the Min Mountains was mainly due to destruction of low-altitude bamboo by agricultural development. Forty-one pandas starved to death in the Pingwu County of Sichuan in 1974 and 1975, when an "arrow" bamboo species had been eliminated from the lower slopes.

In his book *The Giant Pandas of Wolong*, George B. Schaller states: "[The villagers'] advance deprives pandas of food at low elevations and may ultimately confine animals to the upper altitudinal limit of bamboo."

Fuel and housing

Villagers go into high mountain areas to collect wood for fuel and to cut timber for roof shingles and house beams. Firewood and timber for housing are necessary materials, but few can afford to buy from commercial enterprises; it is only a minor offense to cut a winter's supply of fuel oneself. Forest guards know that the peasants need the trees for firewood. Local people have fought and killed guards and each other over forestry rights. Thus, guards are reluctant to stop the cutting of trees even though it is not legal.

Logging

Since 1960 more than half of the region's natural forest vegetation has been destroyed or so disturbed that it no longer provides a suitable panda habitat. Despite simplistic claims that all pandas need is "bamboo and peace," pandas need more than bamboo. They also need large trees to use for scent-marking and sheltered maternity dens. Some conservationists suggest selective felling of trees—leaving those conifers that regenerate easily such as pine, spruce, fir, yew, and birch. Large conifers could be left as den sites. And the shade of the remaining larger trees would ensure that the bamboo roots could regenerate after flowering.

Logging in the pandas' forests has been a problem since the early twentieth century. Sometimes tree cutting was selective. At other times, the elimination of trees was total. In

Wolong, logging began in 1916 and reached a peak between 1961 and 1975, robbing the reserves not only of trees but also the peaceful atmosphere. At this time the government stopped logging in that area in order to preserve the pandas' habitat.

Bamboo trees normally survive logging, but their growth, shape, and condition are affected by the removal of the forest canopy. Without it, bamboo grows shorter, denser, and drier; it is known that pandas spend less time in excessively logged areas. This may be because the bamboo is not as tasty or nutritious or because the altered stems are harder to select and hold in their paws.

Trapping

As people move higher into mountain areas, another problem plagues the pandas. They often become entangled in the snares that people set to trap musk deer. The male musk deer is valuable for its scent gland (or pod), which is used in the manufacture of expensive perfumes and in medicines. Each pod contains about 25 grams of musk—worth over $1,000. It is the living equivalent of gold. (Used in over one hundred medicines, musk is said to cure asthma, typhoid, impotence, pneumonia, and other problems.) For people whose monthly wage is $30 to $50, trap-

A section of a Wolong hillside is stripped of trees to allow for terrace farming.

ping musk deer has an irresistible appeal. Accidental entrapment of pandas is a major cause of the recent, sudden decline in panda numbers. In Wolong, the 1974 census counted 145 pandas; by 1986 the count was only 72.

Tourism

Tourism is an additional threat to panda habitat. Many tourists are eager to see the scenic beauty of western Sichuan. Glacial lakes, spectacular waterfalls, and winding valley floors can be seen in Jiuzhaigon, the first panda reserve open to tourists. While tourism generates jobs and much needed income, it also brings cars, hotels, buses, trails, waste disposal problems, and habitat disturbance.

Bamboo die-off

Nature itself is a factor that threatens the survival of pandas. Bamboo is unusual in that the plant flowers in cycles of 15 to 120 years. After it blooms, every plant of that species in that area dies. The cycle must then begin again in stages from seeds to shoots to plants. It takes up to twenty years to regrow bamboo to mature size from seed. (Bamboo also reproduces by sending out shoots from rootlike rhizomes, which are horizontal roots under or along the ground.)

Mature bamboo trees flourish in this forest in China.

Periodic bamboo die-off threatens the panda population with starvation. When die-offs occurred long ago, pandas would roam to areas where different but still edible types of bamboo grew. But now, roaming pandas find farms and villages instead of bamboo. Because bamboo constitutes 99 percent of the panda's diet, the plant is critical to the panda's survival in the wild.

It is common for several bamboo species to flower during any given year. Usually flowering happens locally—a few clumps, a patch, occasionally a whole mountainside. Generally, the plant loses all its leaves during the winter prior to flowering, blossoms appear in spring, and the plant dies the same year. Therefore, flowering can be predicted a year in advance by the failure of the plants to grow new shoots.

When bamboo blossom is widespread and simultaneous, the occurrence is called "periodic synchronous." This mass flowering of bamboo is a spectacular event. The genetic and environmental reasons for such synchrony are a mystery. During the 1970s and 1980s, there was widespread flowering, with harsh consequences for many pandas.

Mass flowering

Giant pandas favor three bamboo varieties—umbrella, arrow, and fountain—that are available in Wolong and other range areas. There are several subspecies in each variety. In the recent past, umbrella bamboo has flowered in various parts of the Min Mountains of northern Sichuan. For example, between 1974 and 1976, an area of two thousand square miles, or 40 percent of the pandas' total range, flowered. According to the surveys, there may have been at least three species flowering, but because the flowers are similar, this was overlooked.

In 1975 and 1976, another umbrella bamboo mass flowering struck. This time, over 80 percent of the Wanglang Reserve, all but three small valleys and a few scattered patches, was affected. Sometimes a species will flower above the elevation of 8,500 feet one year. Six or seven years later, this same species will flower below that elevation. The 1974–76 mass flowering and resulting loss of bamboo plants caused 138 giant pandas to starve to death.

In the February 1990 *Discover* magazine, author Pat Shipman states: "To make matters worse, the animals that are most likely to starve are breeding-age females that are pregnant or nursing, since they have the highest nutritional needs."

The arrow species has flowered in Wolong at intervals of forty-two and forty-eight years, most recently in 1893, 1935, and 1983. Surveys in late 1983 showed that 90 percent or more of both arrow and fountain bamboo had died in the affected areas throughout Wolong, as well as in other parts of the Qionglai Mountains.

The panda's survival depends on how much bamboo is available. If there is only one bamboo species, flowering and die-off of that species dramatically alters the habitat. However, some bamboo may not be affected. Patchy flowering allows pandas to still obtain food by making minor adjustments in their travels.

This panda is settling in for a feast amidst a clump of bamboo.

George B. Schaller states that pandas have a better chance at survival where more than one bamboo species is available. "In most areas . . . 2 or more bamboo species—as many as 13 in the Liang Mountains—grow at the same or different elevations. By shifting at most a kilometer or two, pandas once had access to an alternative bamboo species in the event that one died." But mere signs of a bamboo species and its availability as *edible* bamboo are two different things. According to Schaller:

> Seedlings grow slowly at elevations of 2,000 m [6,600 feet] and above, attaining a height of only 10 cm [4 inches] by the end of the first year and 50 cm [20 inches] by the fifth year; stems may require 10–15 years to attain full height and diameter. Covered by snow, such seedlings may be virtually unavailable to pandas for several months.

Saving the panda

During the 1983 mass flowering, many pandas were saved from starvation because of two government projects. First, tons of cooked meat were set out in the rugged mountains. Because they were starving, the pandas ate roasted pork chops and goat flesh as a bamboo substitute. Also, more than a ton of pig bones, sheep heads, and other waste parts of butchered animals had been scattered to lure pandas down into umbrella bamboo areas. Second, new bamboo was planted in isolated areas.

During the 1983 flowering in Sichuan Province, there were 125 professional observers patrolling the wilderness areas and monitoring the condition of surviving pandas. As many as five hundred additional people were under one-year contracts to aid in the rescue operation. Rescue workers numbered more than one thousand nationwide.

In the Qionglai Mountains, flowering of the arrow bamboo also reached a peak in 1983. According to official records, 62 dead pandas were found; of 108 pandas taken into captivity, 33 died and 35 were released into areas with abundant bamboo; the remaining 40 were kept in captivity.

Bamboo die-off does serve as a natural check on panda populations by weeding out old and sick animals. Mass flowering and subsequent population thinning would occur regardless of human disturbances. And it is possible that flowering and die-off has a beneficial consequence in that it forces pandas to migrate, introducing greater genetic variation in mates. But a 1987 World Wildlife Fund news release stated: "Satellite images reveal that forest clearance for agriculture will be the main cause of panda extinction, not lack of food through bamboo flowering."

To avoid possible starvation during the periodic mass flowering and die-offs of the bamboo, pandas must be able either to switch to another bamboo species or to immigrate to an unaffected area on their own. With so much land now being appropriated by humans, emigration is not always possible.

Mountains isolate pandas

Most panda populations are isolated, confined to high ridges, and hemmed in by farming. As pandas become isolated in small reserves, their movement to find new mates or to escape bamboo die-offs is restricted. Even the largest panda population, in Wolong, comprises only 130 to 150 animals; the average in secluded areas is 20 to 50. The smaller the population, the more vulnerable it is to environmental stresses, natural disasters, and the weakening effects of inbreeding.

The panda is unique: Its reproductive rate is low, its habitat is restricted, and its population is small. Pandas are highly conservative animals. Creatures of habit, pandas stay comfortably within their range. They stay near water and would rather travel on level trails than climb steep ridges. Only the threat of starvation will force a panda to abandon its familiar territory. So they remain for the most part in isolated pockets, separated from others of their kind by railways, roads, farmland, and clear-felled forests.

Importance of the Wolong Natural Reserve

Those dedicated to panda research have a goal to preserve the existing populations and to reestablish the species in other suitable habitats. To offset human encroachment into panda habitat, the Chinese government has set aside areas where bamboo flourishes and where giant pandas are known to survive.

The first two reserves, established in 1963, are both in Sichuan Province. By the 1980s there were approximately a dozen protected areas that housed about half of all surviving pandas. The largest is Wolong Reserve, established in 1975, which covers around 785 square miles, almost one-fourth the size of Yellowstone National Park.

The Wolong Reserve was established to preserve the panda and its habitat indefinitely. The entrance to the Wolong Reserve, at 6,400 feet, is about eighty miles from Chengdu. The first view of the preserve reveals a large hydroelectric station and a dam. Fields cover the valley floor and spread up the mountainsides. The forest grows only on the steepest pitches and highest ridges.

The center's primary purpose is to study the environment and behavior of free-living giant pandas, to establish an emergency plan for natural disasters such as mass flow-

In the Wolong Reserve, photographers capture on film a panda walking behind a native guide.

ering, and to observe pandas in captivity. But although Wolong Reserve was designated a protected area in 1975, giant pandas do share it with humans. Walter A. Taylor reports in the July 2, 1984, *U.S. News & World Report*:

> Yet 1,800 people, mostly ethnic Tibetans, still live in the preserve, logging trucks still rumble down narrow mountain roads and blasting work still goes on at the site of a new, 160,000-kilowatt hydroelectric plant just 6 miles away.

This ecological damage to the preserve was unavoidable, according to industrial and agricultural advocates who said additional power was necessary for development of the region. These human activities prevent the reclusive pandas from venturing to lower elevations of the preserve, where they could find alternative types of bamboo to eat.

An Emergency Plan

After the 1983 mass flowering, the Chinese government became deeply concerned with saving starving pandas. They prepared an emergency plan that included:

> 1. Building holding stations to rehabilitate starving pandas for eventual release into the wild;
>
> 2. Forming a committee in every affected county to supervise the rescue work;
>
> 3. Assigning teams of four to six people to locate and move starving pandas; providing food such as meat, corn, and sugarcane to pandas near human habitations, making it unnecessary to capture them; and transferring pandas to new habitats with ample bamboo;
>
> 4. Publicizing rescue efforts and offering rewards of $100 to anyone who finds a starving panda and aids in its rescue;
>
> 5. Prohibiting the cutting of bamboo by local people in or near panda habitat.

However, the emergency plan will not eliminate the basic problem of mass flowering. Because seedlings need time to grow tall enough to provide pandas with food, the Chinese government must anticipate a long, sustained conservation effort.

One possible solution is to provide every panda population with at least two easily accessible species of bamboo.

This can be done by cultivating bamboo at lower elevations where bamboo die-off has occurred, by planting seeds or roots, and by preserving existing stands.

Solutions to aid pandas

In the September 1989 issue of *Discover*, Edward Dolnick writes about the disadvantage pandas in some reserves face:

> In 8 of the 12 reserves pandas are . . . outnumbered by people, in one case by 10,000 people to 40 pandas [in Gansu Province]. These people, mainly of Tibetan descent, are ethnic minorities and as such are exempt from China's "one child policy." As their numbers grow, villagers clear more land for farming.

As they do elsewhere in China, these villagers pilfer the forest to obtain wood for heating and cooking and building their homes. One proposal would resettle the villagers—but this is a hugely expensive prospect. For instance, in 1986 the Chinese government spent about $370,000 to resettle the three hundred people living and farming within the Tangjiahe Reserve.

Security for a greater number of pandas is needed. Some solutions include: expanding existing reserves; creating new reserves; preserving or reestablishing habitat corridors to eliminate inbreeding; monitoring plans whereby animal populations may be shifted to other locations. All of these solutions are being implemented in a 1992 ten-year plan by China's State Council.

With its limited diet, slow reproduction cycle, and localized habitat, the giant panda has been called a "living blueprint for extinction." One way researchers are working to change this extinction pattern is through captive breeding programs.

4

Pandas in Captivity

APPROXIMATELY 120 PANDAS live in zoos and breeding facilities around the world. Most of these captive pandas live in China. In 1997, only twenty of the rare animals lived in zoos outside China, in seven countries: United States (three); Japan (six); Mexico (four); Spain (two); France (one); Germany (two); and Korea (two). Currently, giant pandas cannot be taken out of China except for authorized breeding research projects.

"The Chinese, through many press releases and scientific papers, have stated that the plight of the giant panda could be extinction if something is not done immediately," Doug Myers, executive director of the Zoological Society of San Diego, said in the April 19, 1993, *San Diego Union-Tribune*. As fears over possible extinction of giant pandas grow, China becomes increasingly interested in seeking outside help to improve the success rate of breeding animals in captivity.

Successful breeding will take cooperation

Zoo officials in the United States envision a time when several zoos will work closely together to lend and breed their pandas. Ultimately such cooperation would include temporary transfers of the animals to a breeding center where pandas would be clustered together during the spring mating season, allowing a female her choice of several mates and increasing the chances of conception.

Breeding captive pandas must be considered so far unsuccessful even in comparison with the breeding of other

In China's Beijing Zoo, this captive panda appears to be smiling at visitors.

endangered species. Of all the countries involved in breeding captive pandas, China has produced the most cubs. However, even in China, 70 percent of captive female pandas do not go into heat at all, and 90 percent of males refuse to mate. Most of the births have come from just a few individuals.

Transportation out of China

In spite of unsuccessful captive breeding efforts of the giant panda, the process is still seen as a last resort to head off the extinction of this rare animal. In September 1996, the first U.S. scientific panda breeding research project began at the San Diego Zoo. (Past loans have been for temporary exhibition only.) The People's Republic of China transferred to the zoo a pair of giant pandas on loan for a twelve-year project.

Bai Yun (White Cloud), the female, born September 7, 1991, is active and weighs about two hundred pounds. Bai Yun was the first cub born at the Wolong Giant Panda Conservation Center. She was raised by her mother, Dong Dong.

Shi Shi (Rock), the male, was born in the wild in China's Sichuan Province sometime between 1982 and 1986. Chinese villagers found him in March 1992. He had multiple slash wounds on his body, probably incurred in a mating-season scuffle with another panda. The villagers rescued him and took him to the conservation center. Shi Shi recovered from his wounds, but after being cared for by humans for so long, he could not be returned to the wild.

Bai Yun's and Shi Shi's 6,000-mile journey to the San Diego Zoo began at their mountain enclosure in the Wolong Giant Panda Conservation Center. Before they left, the pair spent ten days in quarantine to ensure that they were not carrying any diseases and were healthy enough to

While awaiting transportation out of China, this panda relaxes during a ten-day quarantine.

be transported. The pandas were not sedated en route. They ate bamboo, drank bottled water, and slept during the flight. Doug Myers, along with a nine-member team of zoo employees and three Chinese handlers, accompanied the pandas on their ten-hour plane trip.

Captivity in the San Diego Zoo

Once the pandas arrived at the San Diego Zoo, they were separated and, out of public view, spent fifty-one more days in quarantine to buffer them from any illnesses they might acquire from the zoo population and vice versa.

Before the pandas went on public exhibit, they were anesthetized and taken by van to the zoo hospital. There, they were weighed and measured and blood was drawn. A team of eighteen medical experts examined them from snout to tail and declared them in good health. *San Diego Union-Tribune* staff writer Pat Flynn describes other parts of their physical exam:

> The animals also were given dental exams and electrocardiograms [heart tests]. Scent gland tissue was collected and hair and urine samples were taken. Ultrasounds [silent vibrations] were taken of their hearts and abdomens, and radiographs [X rays] made of the abdomen, chest and major joints. In addition, their eyes, ears, noses and throats were checked, lymph nodes and abdomens palpitated [vibrated], hearts and lungs listened to, feet and claws looked at, and reproductive organs examined.

The purpose of the exam was to give zoo veterinarians a baseline profile of the animals' health to compare against any future changes.

The pandas' zoo home includes several bedrooms, a maternity room, heated floors, video monitoring equipment in each room, and a small laboratory. Adjacent to their exhibit, the pandas have a 9,000-square-foot exercise yard. To provide food for the pandas, four different varieties of bamboo are grown on the San Diego Zoo grounds and in a jointly administered local wildlife preserve. The pandas' favorites are the arrow and umbrella bamboo plants.

John Michel, leader of the zoo's panda team, describes the pandas' reaction to their new home:

In her outdoor quarters at the San Diego Zoo, the female Bai Yun delights visitors.

They're divulging their personalities to us. Bai Yun was given additional access to an outside area, a grassy area with misters on. She was out the door in about 10 seconds to check it out, but then she went right back inside. I thought, "Why didn't she like that?" But then she came back out with some bamboo and had a picnic. Bai Yun responds to her name by walking toward us. Shi Shi is a dignified older gentleman [about sixteen years old]. He is more sedate by comparison. He responds to us by opening one eye. This guy is Mr. Laid-back. He's very, very relaxed.

Roughly half of the pandas' time is spent sleeping, and much of the rest is spent eating. They are fed three times a day—each consumes about eight pounds of bamboo and loaves of bread that the keepers bake daily. Their diet also includes milk and certain root vegetables, like carrots and turnips. They eat for fifteen minutes to an hour and then sleep. When they wake up, they are hungry again.

Five-year-old Bai Yun is far more adventurous than her older mate. In her garden area she climbs a chain-link fence, splashes water, and plays with bamboo shoots. In comparison, Shi Shi is more contemplative. Michel describes the serene Shi Shi: "He likes to sit there and assess his surroundings. If he had a pipe, he'd be smoking it. That's what it seems like to me."

The pandas' behavior has been constantly monitored since their arrival, either by video camera or researchers assigned to the exhibit. When the pandas are on exhibit to the public, about two hundred people at a time can watch them from a three-tiered viewing area. Bai Yun and Shi Shi have side-by-side but separate outdoor enclosures. Zoo employees instruct visitors not to be noisy or rowdy around the rare animals.

Panda personality

Giant pandas project vulnerability and charm, and people tend to see only that image—and not the wild animal. Pandas in zoos are seen playfully chasing a ball, climbing trees, splashing in water, and relaxing or sleeping against a tree—all of which make the animals humanlike. However, a panda is powerful and potentially dangerous, and in order to maintain its lovable impression, its moods are not always truthfully reported. Keepers have been seriously mauled in Chicago, London, and Washington zoos—events that do not receive much publicity. According to George B. Schaller: "Since only thirty-eight pandas lived in zoos outside China between 1937 and the early 1980s, pandas have inflicted proportionately more serious injuries than any other captive species except elephants."

Efforts to breed captive pandas naturally

Natural breeding of captive pandas was first attempted in China in 1955 and was unsuccessful for eight years. Finally, in 1963 Ming Ming, the first captive-bred giant panda, was born in Beijing Zoo. People concerned about panda survival were jubilant. They thought they had found the answer to captive breeding. The breeding program continued. Unfortunately, fourteen years later, only ten pregnancies had occurred in Beijing (four single births and six pairs of twins). Of the sixteen babies, only seven survived to adulthood.

The Chapultepec Zoo in Mexico City is the only park outside China to have successfully bred pandas naturally in captivity. In 1981 a cub, Tohui, was born and is still alive. Of eight pandas born at this zoo, four are still living.

Several problems make panda reproduction in captivity difficult. First, females ovulate only once a year and their peak receptivity to mating lasts only two-to-five days. Second, captive males usually don't show much interest in mating. Thus, a harmonious courtship is sometimes difficult to achieve.

Nevertheless, scientists at the San Diego Zoo are hopeful that Bai Yun will conceive. And if she does, they want to follow the development of the baby inside Bai Yun's uterus via ultrasound; they have practiced procedures to familiarize and desensitize her to human examination, made easier by the female's docility.

Pandas are not necessarily cooperative when they are brought together, however. Some will squabble. Some will

To prepare Bai Yun for future sonograms, San Diego Zoo's lead panda keeper John Michel uses a cordless electric shaver to remove hair from a small patch on her stomach. Keeper Lety Plasencia distracts the panda with food.

show disinterest. In the *San Diego Union-Tribune*, Ron Swaisgood, a postdoctoral student at the zoo's Center for the Reproduction of Endangered Species (CRES), describes how researchers will know when the time is right to let the two pandas into the same enclosure.

> Their behavior is not very subtle. In the wild, males go to the top of a ridge and go through a medley of sounds, roars and growls. We don't know if it's meant to keep other males away or to attract females. Females vocalize incessantly [continuously]. They bark like a dog, chirp like a bird, bleat like a goat and do a lot of moaning.

A scientific way of pinpointing the best time for the female to get pregnant is to analyze daily samples of her urine. Estrogen concentrations in the urine can be measured, and from that, ovulation time can be determined.

Mating opportunity elapses

For a number of weeks the two pandas sniffed each other through a wire doorway of their enclosures. Later they were placed in the same enclosure for short visits. When the proper time for mating came about, Bai Yun and Shi Shi were put together. A restless Bai Yun indicated her interest when she rejected food. Bai Yun had also become obsessed with leaving scent marks on logs, trees, rocks, and everywhere else. In addition, her hormone levels indicated that the time was right to bring the two pandas together.

Bai Yun and Shi Shi were paired twice a day from 8:00 A.M. to 10:00 A.M. and 4:00 P.M. to 6:00 P.M. Unfortunately, Shi Shi seemed uninterested in Bai Yun. The male warded Bai Yun off and treated her like an intruder into his space. Consequently, the San Diego giant pandas did not mate in spring 1997. They will not have another opportunity to mate until spring 1998.

However, the San Diego researchers were optimistic regarding other results of their reproductive study. The female showed interest in mating, measured high hormone levels, and demonstrated a change in behavior. The main purpose in bringing the giant pandas to the zoo was to gain understanding of their reproductive habits.

Neither Shi Shi nor Bai Yun has been bred successfully in captivity. However, Shi Shi may have fathered a cub or two before he was taken from the wild in 1992. If the two fail to breed naturally, panda veterinarians plan to use artificial insemination. They will use either Shi Shi's sperm or frozen sperm from pandas in European zoos. But frozen sperm is considered a poor substitute because the freezing process slows down the sperm's motility.

At the San Diego Zoo, Shi Shi (left) and Bai Yun rub noses through a wire gate. Zookeepers are hopeful that the two will eventually mate.

Artificial insemination

The dismal breeding record of pandas in zoos has been largely blamed on the male's lack of interest in mating. Faced with these natural breeding failures, Chinese zoos and breeding centers have mostly resorted to artificial insemination. Because the female panda's ovulation period is so short, zookeepers frequently inseminate her artificially even though she may have mated naturally.

*Researchers at the
Wolong Wildlife
Protection Zone
artificially inseminate a
sedated panda. This
measure is taken to
help ensure
reproduction of the
endangered panda.*

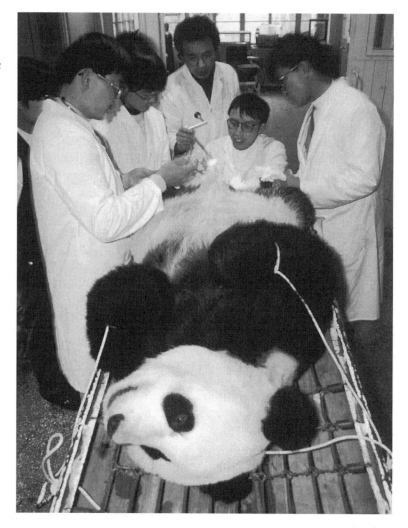

Panda scientists do not want to waste a pregnancy opportunity. To increase the female's chances of conceiving, zoos in China inseminate with sperm from multiple donors. This means researchers do not immediately know which male was the father, but geneticists can later use DNA in hair follicles to determine paternity. This information is necessary in order to avoid future inbreeding.

In 1978, Beijing Zoo was the first institution with a successful panda birth using artificial insemination. Outside China, the first two cubs conceived by artificial insemination were born in 1982 to Shao Shao in Madrid Zoo. The semen for the Madrid breeding was from London Zoo's panda, Chia Chia—not from Chang Chang, her in-residence mate, whose attempts at mating proved unsuccessful.

Test-tube pandas

The National Zoo in Washington, D.C., is hoping to try a new technique to increase panda population artificially. After Ling-Ling, their female giant panda, died on December 30, 1992, zoo officials harvested a hundred eggs from her ovaries. The eggs are being kept in frozen storage. In the future, they hope to fertilize some of these eggs with sperm from Hsing-Hsing, Ling-Ling's zoo mate since 1972.

In 1996, Chinese scientists announced a plan to produce the world's first test-tube panda through in vitro fertilization (IVF). The plan is to remove an ovary from a dead female panda and extract and cultivate the eggs. When an egg is mature, it will be fertilized with sperm. Placed in a test tube, the fertilized egg will be nurtured until an embryo forms. The embryo will be frozen in liquid nitrogen until a suitable panda host is found. The panda embryo transplant experiments are projected to begin in 1999. First, however, IVF will be refined using black bears.

This IVF project has stirred much debate. In the June 14, 1996, issue of *Science*, Zhou Meiyue reports:

> IVF proponents say that the panda population has declined to the point that new technologies must be found to ward off panda extinction. But opponents say that the reproductive rates of wild pandas, although low, are sufficient to preserve the species if more is done to protect their habitat.

These disagreements extend to officials from both sides—captive breeding

Hsing-Hsing peers down at Ling-Ling at the National Zoo. The two were zoo mates for twenty years, but none of their five offspring lived very long.

versus wildlife preservation and conservation—who compete for limited resources. George B. Schaller, an opponent of capturing pandas from the wild to use for breeding in captivity, was relentless in his drive to release two pandas from the Wolong Research Center that had been captured in his study area. In *The Last Panda*, he presents his argument on moral grounds:

> Their [pandas'] dignity has been taken away. Was Hua-Hua's [male] future to be electro-ejaculated [forced to discharge semen] once a year instead of struggling with others of his kind for the right to mate? Was Zhen-Zhen's [female] future [only] to be drugged again and again and artificially inseminated? Removed from their culture—their society and pattern of life—their lives would be tranquil but empty, a tragedy.

Finally, after many discussions and meetings, Schaller won the two pandas' release.

Loss of panda lives

Giant pandas have a high level of infant mortality in captivity. Only 39 percent of the Chinese and 40 percent of the non-Chinese captive-born cubs have survived infancy. In comparison, survival of captive brown bear cubs is 83 percent and for the captive black bear, 78 percent. All attempts at hand rearing panda cubs before one month old have failed.

At the National Zoo in Washington, D.C., all attempts to breed Ling-Ling and Hsing-Hsing ended in disappointment. All five of their offspring either were stillborn or died from infections within hours of their births.

Monetary deals

Giant pandas are protected under the Endangered Species Act of 1973 and by international treaty. Over 130 nations have signed the Convention on International Trade in Endangered Species (CITES), an international treaty regulating or banning trade in designated animal parts or products as well as live importation. Since pandas were listed in 1984, an import permit is required to bring them into the United States.

A panda from China arrives in Canada enroute to the Calgary Zoo.

Bringing giant pandas to the United States is a slow and expensive process. Doug Myers describes the San Diego Zoo's acquisition of two pandas as "a five-year roller-coaster ride" and a "very frustrating experience." As home to the renowned Center for the Reproduction of Endangered Species (CRES), the San Diego Zoo was the site of the Chinese government's proposal to transfer a pair of giant pandas in hopes that CRES could help forestall its extinction. Using captive breeding programs, CRES has been successful in breeding endangered species such as the Przewalski wild horse, the oryx, the California condor, the Bali mynah, the Plains bison and others. By 1997, a total of twenty species had an increased captive population.

In some cases, like the California condor, the species are slowly being released back into the wild. In other cases, their numbers are steadily growing due to special breeding programs.

Over $3 million was spent on the panda project before the breeding pair even arrived in San Diego. These expenses included $1 million for the zoo's open-moated panda habitat exhibit (which then stood empty for three years). Further expenses involved travel costs for scientists who journeyed repeatedly to China for four years, legal fees, and staff time required to complete permit applications.

Panda loan negotiation

The panda loan was first negotiated in October 1992. From the start it was plagued by delays. First, U.S. Fish and Wildlife Service (FWS) officials insisted on a revised scientific research proposal. In April 1993, the FWS returned the zoo's five-hundred-page import application asking for more information and documentation. The zoo's revised permit application was ultimately denied in September 1993 by the Department of the Interior—a major blow to the zoo—primarily because of concern that accepting wild-born animals would encourage poaching in China.

The initial proposal was a request to help pandas reproduce in captivity and assist them in the wild. After fifteen months of rewriting, the permit application was revised to emphasize research opportunities. Specifically, there would be a scientific study on how pandas use gel-like scent markings to communicate readiness to mate within their territories. This information will help all zoos to improve captive breeding of giant pandas, and hopefully benefit the dwindling wild panda population.

During this frustrating time, Jeff Jouett, spokesman for the Zoological Society of San Diego, which operates the zoo, stated, "We are not giving up on pandas. We are committed to participating in the international panda rescue effort, and we will do that by whatever means we are allowed."

The long-term loan program has given San Diego Zoo the distinction of being the first U.S. zoo to acquire pandas for a breeding research experiment. The money spent un-locking the secrets of panda biology and saving the species from extinction is offset by increased zoo attendance and the resulting sale of panda souvenirs and books. Because of the magnetic attraction of the rare giant pandas, public attention is also drawn to the panda's plight and affects sentiment toward other endangered species. Awareness encourages public action.

The long-sought importation permit for pandas to come to the United States was finally issued in January 1995. But, in China, various agencies battled for the next eighteen months over which would receive the money in exchange for the animals. It took six months of personal appeals—letters and private meetings between California senator Dianne Feinstein and Chinese president Jiang Zemin—before an export permit was approved.

Agreements

During the twelve-year period that the pandas will be at the zoo, the Zoological Society of San Diego has agreed to contribute $1 million annually to China. In addition, the society will provide scientific assistance (such as equipment sharing and expertise) to Chinese scientists. The money is expected to come from the anticipated increase in zoo attendance. These conservation funds will specifically go to three of China's new habitat reserves in Sichuan Province—Wujiao, Baodinggon, and Yele. This added land would create corridors between isolated islands of panda territory, allowing for expanded bamboo foraging and healthy crossbreeding. This infusion of money into China's panda preservation efforts could hopefully greatly improve the pandas' chances in the wild.

Besides the $1 million annual donation, the zoo pledged to pay up to $600,000 for each cub that survives for at least six months. (The cub remains the property of China.) The U.S. Fish and Wildlife Service has developed a national policy on panda importation to ensure that other zoos follow San Diego's lead in stressing habitat conservation and panda research as the main focus of any loans.

In 1995 the American Zoo and Aquarium Association organized a cluster of twenty-eight zoos that will share in the research and display of any future pandas allowed into the United States. The association would like China to send ten to fifteen pandas to U.S. zoos over the next decade. To make sure the imports are nonprofit, permits will specify that funds generated from the panda loan in excess of the operational costs of the exhibit will be used to fund recovery and conservation programs in China and North America. The FWS insists that the profits go back to the pandas, or the pandas cannot come into the United States. San Diego Zoo spokesman Jeff Jouett stresses the need for more pandas in the United States:

At a first meeting without fences separating them, the male Shi Shi honked, growled, and barked at Bai Yun.

We cannot save the pandas with just two animals in San Diego. China needs the cooperation of more than just the San Diego Zoo. The Chinese have said they need from $50 million to $80 million to put their national plan in place, and that's money that will have to come from all over the world and from more zoos and more cities than San Diego.

Captive-bred giant pandas and captured cubs often adapt well to life in a cage. In the short term, one of the main contributions of captive pandas may be their ability to earn money, thereby contributing to the survival of their wild cousins.

In 1958 Chi Chi netted $2,000 per week on her tour of Europe. Many deals are well-kept secrets, but it is known that in 1990 the Chinese government charged a fee of $300,000 to $600,000 for a three- to six-month loan of a pair of pandas to foreign zoos.

Panda loans involve many scientists

Many people are involved in the San Diego Zoo panda project: behaviorists, endocrinologists, microbiologists, reproductive physiologists, and geneticists, to name a few. Many have been working with Chinese scientists since 1979 as part of the Zoo's Center for the Reproduction of Endangered Species. Their function is to conduct in-depth studies of panda behavior and reproductive biology.

Other organizations involved with the San Diego Zoo panda conservation program include the American Zoo and Aquarium Association, the U.S. Fish and Wildlife Service, the International Union for the Conservation of Nature, World Wildlife Fund, the Chinese Ministry of Forestry, and other Chinese government departments.

Profits from pandas

After the Chinese revolution of 1949, pandas were declared a "national treasure," meaning they could no longer be exported officially to other countries. The Chinese government did on occasion present pandas as gifts, thus making pandas official goodwill ambassadors.

In the 1970s, China began to exploit the political uses of the panda, paralleling a general thaw in its foreign relations policy. Pandas were on loan to zoos in Japan, the United States, England, France, Spain, Mexico, and North Korea. By 1983, a total of twenty-four pandas had been presented as gifts of friendship. Los Angeles Zoo had two pandas on loan during the 1984 Olympics; after the competition, these pandas went on exhibition at the San Francisco Zoo for three months. The period of panda gifts ended in 1985, however, shortly after the extensive bamboo die-off in China.

"Rent-a-panda" deals can be highly profitable for zoos. In 1987–88, San Diego hosted a pair of pandas for about six months. The zoo experienced a 13 percent surge in attendance and netted about $5.4 million in merchandise sales and admission fees during the two-hundred-day stay.

Temporary panda visits, such as the 108-day stay at the Los Angeles Zoo, create controversy. Some feel that such exhibits promote public concern for the animals and are worth the risk to the animals because the money earned goes toward China's panda conservation efforts. Those opposed say zoos just want to make money off the pandas and that the pandas' health and safety are jeopardized during moving. They point out that a female on loan may miss the opportunity to mate. George B. Schaller is one of those opposed to panda exhibits. In *The Last Panda*, he states:

> If the millions of dollars that have been raised from loans were spent on anti-poaching and forest protection measures instead of on the construction and maintenance of walls around pandas, the future of the species would be brighter.

Opposition to managing pandas in zoos

In response to increasing clamor from (poorly prepared) zoos in the United States and elsewhere for (potentially profitable) panda exhibits, the U.S. Fish and Wildlife Service announced in June 1988 the suspension of all import licenses for pandas. In 1990 a worldwide temporary moratorium on all panda loans was imposed, and by 1993 U.S. officials had made the ban permanent. But this ban did not affect San Diego's application, which was in progress before the ban was implemented. In *The Last Panda*, George B. Schaller expresses his opposition to captive pandas in China's zoos:

> Hunched in corners of their iron-barred cages, most [pandas] would pass their years viewed by an enthusiastic public that sees only a clownish face, not the haunting image of a

dying species. Few of these pandas would ever breed. However, if most of those that were rescued after the [1983] bamboo die-off were given their liberty they would perhaps replenish the forests.

In June 1993, the World Wildlife Fund asked the U.S. Fish and Wildlife Service to deny the San Diego Zoo a permit to import two giant pandas from China for a breeding program. The WWF perceived the loan as premature. Ginette Hemley, director of the WWF's wildlife trade monitoring program, said that San Diego should wait a year or more until an international advisory group and international breeding program was organized. The WWF said only pandas born in captivity should be used in long-term loans, and the two pandas chosen for the loan had been rescued in the wild. One had been near death from starvation, and the other had been slashed in a fight; however, both had been in a reserve since 1992. The *San Diego Union-Tribune* reported Jeff Jouett's response:

Pandas Qing Qing (left) and Quan Quan play at a Toronto Zoo during their one-hundred-day loan from China.

The World Wildlife Fund is a respected conservation organization that has done a great deal for pandas over the last 30 years. But panda populations have continued to decline for the past 30 years, [so] what they are doing doesn't seem to be working. . . . It would be a real shame if panda politics are the deciding factors. If that happens, the pandas would be the losers.

In January of 1995, after the permit was finally granted, critics still strongly opposed the San Diego project. "As far as the Humane Society of the United States (HSUS) is concerned, any loan is still a rent-a-panda loan for entertainment and for gate numbers to go up for the zoo," Richard Farinato, director of the HSUS's captive wildlife protection program, was quoted saying in the *San Diego Union-Tribune.*

However, John W. Grandy, vice president of the HSUS Wildlife and Habitat Protection, later softened the Humane Society's stance:

Indeed the proposal [Interior Secretary Bruce] Babbitt has approved is unique because it would at least attempt to benefit the animals themselves and guarantee money for conservation. This is a standard to which all zoos should adhere for all animals under their care.

Although short-term exhibition loans of pandas are still opposed by the WWF, changing circumstances have altered their position regarding long-term breeding loans. Long-term breeding loans may now meet with their approval if they are reviewed and accepted by the American Zoo and Aquarium Association and the Chinese Association of Zoological Gardens. Primarily, this change of heart stems from hope that breeding projects by zoos outside China will be more successful.

Endangered species conservationists and many panda supporters are hopeful that U.S. breeding experiments will aid the pandas in reproducing in captivity. Success in this area may be the last hope to save the species from extinction.

5

China's Action Plans to Save the Panda

THE SURVIVAL OF the giant panda in the wild is in grave doubt. In 1980, in an attempt to save its remaining populations, the Chinese government agreed to cooperate with the World Wildlife Fund (WWF) on a collaborative panda research project. A joint committee of six members—three from China and three from the World Wildlife Fund—was formed. Two panda experts led the group: Dr. George B. Schaller, noted ecologist and director of Wildlife Conservation International of the New York Zoological Society, represented the WWF and Hu Jinchu, associate professor of biology at Nanchong Normal College in Sichuan, represented China.

Action plans

Between 1980 and 1992, several plans were tried, discarded, and refined. The first action plan, in 1980, included not only building a research center in Wolong equipped with laboratories, a breeding facility, a veterinary hospital, and a panda nursery, but also instituting a field research project headed by George B. Schaller and Hu Jinchu. From the beginning, Schaller reported that the project was besieged with communication problems.

One problem entailed the WWF's blatant promotion of the project, which was viewed by many in China as a publicity campaign to benefit WWF. World Wildlife Fund's aggressive marketing of its interests (panda gold coins, postage stamps) and its aversion to sharing public recognition eroded Chinese trust in the project. And the partnership was jeopardized by a number of other events, including failure to invite the Ministry of Forestry and the Chinese Academy of Sciences to a ceremonial signing; the WWF's request that the head of the Chinese delegation sign a nonapproved addendum; China's request for lavish high-technology equipment; and little flexibility in China's demands. The spirit of cooperation collapsed.

By 1984, at a joint meeting of Sichuan and Wolong officials, Schaller said he was "sick at heart and angry." The action plan of the previous four years had yielded dismal results. Schaller listed several sources of trouble: disastrous decisions by the Wolong leadership; constant interference in research and in pandas' lives; no controls over poaching; no senior staff in the research center assigned to use the delicate equipment provided by the WWF; and broken equipment. Schaller suggested cleaning house (assigning new, competent workers), monthly meetings, and designated job responsibilities.

A sign marked with the symbol of a panda points the way to the Wolong Natural Reserve.

Schaller's field research ended in January 1985. By the end of 1987, seven of the eight pandas in his study were either dead or their radios had ceased to function, shrouding their lives in mystery. Research in both Wolong and Tangjiahe Reserves had ceased, and the research bases were deserted. However, since 1984, Schaller's research has continued in another province, the Qin Ling Mountains of Shaanxi Province, by zoologists Pan Wenshi and Lü Zhi.

New plans

In 1992, China's State Council approved a new ten-year plan entitled "The National Conservation Programme for the Giant Panda and its Habitat" (NCPGP). One-fifth of its $35.7 million budget will be provided by the Chinese government. The WWF has agreed to help the Ministry of Forestry raise the necessary funds to implement the program. The funds come primarily from membership and their budget, which includes marketing ventures, grants, and foundations.

According to the WWF International Country profile of China in 1995, some of the NCPGP activities have already begun:

> Two new reserves were established in 1993—Laoxiancheng in the Shaanxi Province and Anzihe in the Sichuan Province. The Sichuan Forestry Department has begun detailed designs for the 10 proposed reserves in the province. Several existing panda reserves have been upgraded, and a central office to oversee the NCPGP is up and running at the Ministry of Forest[ry] in Beijing. WWF will also start work at the Wanglang Reserve in northern Sichuan's Min Mountains. This is in addition to other on-going WWF-supported activities such as reserve management planning, guard training at Wolong, and the research work of Pan Wenshi, one of China's leading panda experts.

In 1994 the National Environmental Protection Agency in Beijing announced the planning and establishment of the Longmenshan Reserve in Sichuan Province.

> The objectives of this project are to establish a nature reserve in the northern Min Mountains protecting more of the Giant Panda's fragmented range, and with it the high biodiversity associated with this region. This planned reserve covers 970

km², and has been given high priority in the Ministry of Forestry's program to protect the Giant Panda.

A June 1997 WWF work plan includes workshops on panda reintroduction and the feasibility of ecotourism in panda areas, surveys, reserve staff training, monitoring of biodiversity, education and public awareness, community-based conservation activities; and hiring two Chinese researchers to work with Dr. Lü Zhi. Recommendations of the NCPGP include relocating farmers, halting logging in some areas, linking isolated reserves with corridors, doubling the size of reserves, and supporting studies of giant panda breeding in the wild and in zoos. The Chinese government has been working hard to enact these recommendations, but faces its biggest obstacle in changing people's traditional attitudes and practices.

Human settlement poses the greatest threat to the giant panda. Population expansion has steadily pushed the panda from its habitat and human activities destroy that habitat. No attempts to reverse the decline in panda numbers have shown significant effect: Long-term success depends on persuading everyone living in or near a panda habitat that the aims and objectives of the conservation effort are worthwhile.

Educating China's inhabitants

In 1986, an educational campaign was launched in five thousand villages and forest farms throughout Sichuan Province. The intention was to teach farmers and villagers about panda protection, discourage the cutting of bamboo, and advise locals on coping with and aiding starving pandas. To drum up interest, local authorities allocated funds to reimburse peasants for homes or crops damaged by pandas desperate for food after the bamboo had flowered and died.

Researchers transport a wild panda to the Wolong Wildlife Protection Zone in May 1996. Sponsored by China Wildlife Foundation and World Wildlife Foundation, the area is comprised of nearly one million acres. Twenty-six pandas live in the protection zone, which is staffed by thirteen researchers and eight workers.

However, winning the hearts and minds of the Chinese people toward conservation is an enormous task. Much of the wildlife of China was, until recently, valued only as potential ingredients for Chinese medicine. New restrictions aimed at protecting panda habitat have seriously disrupted people's ways of life.

Ideal panda habitat can be described as large interconnecting areas of sloping terrain, adequate stream flow, moderate tree cover, and extensive undergrowth of at least one species of bamboo. The areas should be left undisturbed by dogs, domestic livestock, or human activities. Managing such habitat generally takes two forms: establishing panda reserves, and improving their habitat outside of the reserve system. To accomplish both of these goals, human activities must be limited and reduced.

Within nature reserves, regulations prohibit human settlement, forest cutting, the collection of medicinal plants, domestic animal grazing, and hunting. These rules apply to all citizens. Removing human settlements from reserves is sometimes accomplished by redrawing reserve boundary lines to exclude human settlements. A second, more expensive way is to actually move and resettle established human communities.

Resistance to relocating

After the bamboo famine in 1983, China's Ministry of Forestry made a plan to relocate 100 households (590 people) closest to the panda habitat. They were to be moved from the upper to the lower part of the reserve because no alternative place existed. To entice the minority peoples into resettling, new homes were constructed. Schools, a power plant, and pastureland were planned. But there was limited potential for agriculture in the area and therefore no way for the settlers to make a living.

These moves were not enthusiastically accepted by the Wolong peasants, as reported by Jeff Sommer in *Newsday*, June 1984: Yang, 32, said, "My people have lived here for a long time, as long as anyone remembers. We don't see why we should move for some animals." Li Tiaxing, 35,

said, "We're not moving. We were born here and we're staying here." Thus, most of the new homes stood empty, and the peasants won the first round in the clash of wills.

The Wolong Panda Reserve is still home to peasants who have refused to leave their homes and gardens.

In 1991, three hundred people were relocated from the Tangjiahe Natural Reserve in Qingchuan County of Sichuan Province. The relocation project cost China's Ministry of Forestry $370,000, including compensation for loss of resources, such as walnut trees and orchards, which had to be left behind. Results of this move are not available.

The NCPGP spelled out new directives to safeguard panda habitats outside of the reserves. Hunting and burning of vegetation are banned; bamboo is restocked; migration corridors across roads are identified and protected; and forestry operations and logging are modified or halted so as not to harm pandas.

Modify forestry operations

Deforestation in panda territory has been a big concern for China. Between 1974 and 1992 panda territory had fallen by half, leaving only the six forest fragments in the provinces of Sichuan, Gansu, and Shaanxi. The ten-year plan includes expanding the thirteen existing reserves and creating fourteen new ones. In 1996 the Ministry of Forestry drew up blueprints for an additional nineteen panda protection zones. When completed, about 95 percent of China's wild pandas will be covered by the zones. In the February 1995 *National Geographic*, zoologist Pan Wenshi estimated the cost of this step:

> Ten thousand loggers and farmers now working in these areas would be paid to move out. The entire effort could cost a staggering 80 million dollars. China has budgeted 13 million and hopes the balance will come from international conservation groups.

Pan Wenshi suggests that one source of revenue might come from the new long-term loans of captive pandas to zoos and parks worldwide for breeding purposes. Like the program at the San Diego Zoo, panda loans would last ten years or more, bringing in at least $10 million from each borrower. Pan Wenshi also reports on forestry operations:

> Logging in the Qin Ling mountains has caused one group of 20 pandas to split up and join other groups, with unknown consequences. But in November 1993 the roar of the chain saws ceased: The government has pledged three million dollars to reorganize a local logging company into five separate factories. In them 2,300 former loggers will make paper products, bio-fertilizer, and other goods.

Pan Wenshi describes the environmental conditions of a panda birthing den that he visited with colleague Lü Zhi in August 1993. "At the time, their den was within earshot of logging operations. Snow—a shy mother—had to raise her cub amid the rumble of heavy equipment and blasts of explosives."

Logging guidelines

Acknowledging that not all timber in panda habitat can be left untouched, the conservation team sought to reduce the damage done to the habitat by setting up guidelines under which no new logging will be allowed in panda habitat. Existing logging areas will be gradually reduced and cutting methods changed.

For example, guidelines specify that loggers must selectively leave at least one-third of the forest in place so that natural reseeding can take place. All large hollow trees must be left for panda nursery dens. Loggers must also cut the forest in a designated pattern, leaving panda travel paths and quiet sections to which pandas can retreat during a logging disturbance.

Linking reserves with corridors

Human involvement is essential to save the pandas from extinction. This requires more than preventing their slaughter and the destruction of their habitats. It is necessary that humans control the pandas' genetic future. The WWF emphasizes that isolated populations of pandas need established "corridors" to encourage migration between them.

The Chinese propose to end the isolation of scattered pandas living in pockets within the reserves. To link the separate groups to one another, reserves will be connected by seventeen corridors of flourishing bamboo groves.

A wild panda refreshes itself in a shallow stream of the Shaanxi Province.

Zhou Zhihua of the Ministry of Forestry reasons, "We hold that pandas should live in the wild rather than captivity. Zoos should only serve as a supplement."

Translocation

Replanting suitable bamboo and forest cover can restore panda habitat and reconnect it to other populations with the expectation that outbreeding will follow. But if established corridors are not successful at mixing gene pools, a second strategy has been suggested. This is translocation—that is, capturing pandas in one area and releasing them in another. However, previous experience with the capture and release of giant pandas has been discouraging. Fourteen pandas were captured after mass bamboo flowering in the 1970s and 1980s. When released into the wild in 1986, three of the pandas wore radio collars so researchers could track them. One died, and the other two took up residence close to their original ranges.

Another possible way to add variety to panda gene pools is to capture females in the wild and either artificially inseminate them or transfer embryos from captive females. However, to date this tactic is not practical because captive breeding has not produced viable embryos or reliably successful inseminations.

Maintaining a captive population

Chinese attitudes toward saving the panda differ from most westerners' ideas. "I don't think that [the Chinese would] be truly worried if the panda disappeared from the wild, if there was a decent population in captivity," said George B. Schaller in 1989. "That may be why they're emphasizing captive breeding even though a little bit of habitat management would maintain the species in the wild."

During seven years of research field trips in the Qin Ling Mountains in Shaanxi Province, Beijing University zoologists Pan Wenshi and Lü Zhi discovered that after panda cubs mature, mothers might leave them alone for as long as fifty-two hours. In the past, researchers and hikers assumed that the cubs were abandoned. They would take

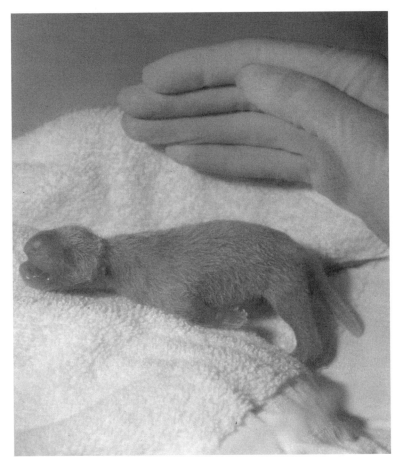

A newborn panda at the National Zoo in Washington, D.C. So far, pandas born in captivity have had a higher mortality rate than those born in the wild.

the orphans to a care center, where they became a part of China's captive breeding program. Of 113 pandas in captivity in various zoos throughout China, thirty-five were taken as cubs from the wild. "These 'rescues' must cease," said Pan Wenshi.

Breeding rate low

The success of the native captive breeding program is severely hampered by inferior facilities, untrained personnel, and little cooperation between institutions holding captive pandas. The breeding rate of captive pandas is low, and the mortality rate of captive-born pandas is high.

There are approximately twenty-three pandas at the China Conservation and Research Center for the Giant

Panda in Wolong. And in fact, Chinese scientists have improved the success rate of captive breeding. Since 1991, natural mating has resulted in eight births at the Wolong center.

A captive breeding program could be a useful tool. But George B. Schaller believes that the program does not need more than eighty animals in captivity:

> We cannot claim to have saved the giant panda if all we end up with is a viable [workable] captive population. The real goal of conservation is to save the species in the wild by means of habitat conservation and maintenance of genetic variation. Captive breeding is only useful for species conservation if it helps to achieve that end and this is only possible if we find ways to release captive-born pandas back into the wild.

Releasing captive-born pandas into the wild

In 1990 author Chris Catton, in *Pandas,* stated his opinion on captive panda breeding and later release:

> By pooling their expertise, Chinese and Western zoologists may succeed in reaching their newly declared goal—a stable captive population. Even if they do, the possibility of successfully releasing pandas bred in captivity into the wild is uncertain. Re-introduction cannot possibly succeed unless the original reasons for the panda's extinction are removed. A re-introduction programme would take more planning, require more political support and be more expensive than a proper programme of protection. With present levels of expertise in captive breeding, the only certain hope of a secure future for the giant panda lies in ensuring adequate protection of the wild population.

Six years later, zoologist Pan Wenshi supported Catton's theory. In the June 14, 1996, issue of *Science* he wrote, "The best way to save pandas is to preserve their habitats and release pandas back to the mountains. Pandas have a much higher rate of survival in their habitats than in zoos."

Tracking

To illustrate his point, Pan Wenshi describes tracking about eighty pandas in the Qin Ling Mountains between 1988 and 1995. During that time, the group of researchers recorded eleven births and only four natural deaths.

Tracking is commonly managed by attaching a radio collar to the panda's neck. The wild panda is first lured into a baited trap, sedated, measured, weighed, and examined. The waterproof radio collar is powered by a fingernail-size battery and will transmit signals for nearly two years. Transmitted signals alert scientists to the panda's location and its activities. Field workers keep tabs on collared animals with a directional antenna, a receiver, and earphones.

The ultimate aim of breeding pandas in captivity is to restock wild populations, either by expanding an existing habitat or stocking a new one. At this writing no captive-born pandas have been released into the wild. A future plan is to release young adult pandas (age five years and older) into forest areas with plentiful bamboo. At this age and size (two hundred pounds), the pandas could find food easily and fend for themselves.

The future of the giant panda

Millions of dollars have been spent to delay the extinction of the giant panda. The Chinese have opened their doors to Western researchers, inviting their expertise in solving the panda's plight. In the September 1989 issue of *Discover*, columnist Edward Dolnick expresses his opinion:

> Despite all the goodwill in the world, the animal [panda] seems headed for oblivion. Why is that bad? Maybe, from an evolutionary standpoint, their number is up and that's all there is to it. It's hard to argue that we need to save pandas because they have enormous economic value. It's hard to argue that we are likely to derive significant scientific and medical benefits from them, as we might from a host of other threatened animals and plants. It's even hard to argue, because pandas are already so few and so isolated, that they have tremendous ecological significance. Their loss certainly wouldn't threaten global well-being in the way that, say, the wholesale destruction of the rain forests would. So why save pandas? In the end the reasons are aesthetic and symbolic. Pandas should be saved just because we like to live in a world that still has exotic animals, even ones we may never see.

"This generation and the next will have to work hard to save the panda," says Hu Jinchu, China's foremost panda

Most experts agree that the future of the giant panda will be severely threatened unless measures are taken to protect the species.

expert. "If not, the panda will be extinct within 100 years." In *Living Treasures*, Tang Xiyang discusses several trends that indicate the danger of pandas becoming extinct:

> People living near panda habitats report seeing fewer pandas than in the past. Surveyors, too, report finding fewer feces, nests, and traces of food indicating the presence of giant pandas. The great majority of giant pandas seen in the wild are adults; very few cubs have been sighted. The reproduction rate of the giant panda is lower than the death rate.

In 1995, National Geographic filmmaker Mark Stouffer spent three months following China's foremost panda protectors, Professor Pan Wenshi and his colleague Lü Zhi. Stouffer says, "The Chinese government has suddenly realized that it doesn't have diamonds but it *does* have pandas. They're a valuable commodity, politically and economically."

The future of giant pandas is linked with the future of the Chinese people. In the first half of the 1980s, George B. Schaller devoted over four years to studying the giant panda in the wild. He sums up his analysis of the study in *The Last Panda*:

> The ultimate responsibility for saving the panda in its natural home rests with China: it alone can implement the measures needed for the animal's protection. The rest of the world must, however, offer guidance, funds, and more support. The gravity of the situation represents both hope and opportunity. But if we fail to make the correct choices now, the last pandas will disappear, leaving us with the nostalgia of a failed epic, and indictment of civilization as destroyer. We cannot recover a lost world.

Glossary

ancestry: Descent or lineage; collective ancestors.

anesthetize: To induce loss of physical sensation by means of a drug.

artificial: Made by humans rather than occurring in nature.

bamboo: A tall treelike tropical grass with hollow, jointed stems.

camouflage: To conceal by blending into the natural background.

captive: Held as a prisoner; under restraint or control.

carcass: An animal's dead body.

chromosome: A cell body, composed of DNA, responsible for determining hereditary characteristics.

collaborate: To work together in a joint effort.

conception: The fusing of an egg and sperm to form a new organism.

conservationist: A person who protects and limits the use of natural resources, including animal and plant life.

corridor: A narrow strip of land connecting two or more areas.

cyclical: Occurring in cycles; a periodic repeating occurrence.

encroach: To intrude or infringe gradually upon the property of another.

endangered: Something that is at risk.

entrepreneur: One who organizes, operates, and assumes the risk of a business venture.

environment: The external circumstances that surround and affect the development of an organism.

fauna: Animal life of a particular region.

fibrous: Tough plant stems.

flora: Plant life of a particular region.

forage: To search for food.

geneticist: A person who studies heredity.

gully: A deep channel cut in the earth by running water.

habitat: The natural environment in which something lives.

inbreed: The continual breeding of closely related individuals.

insemination: To introduce semen into the uterus of a female.

intervene: To come between, change, or delay an event.

migrate: To move regularly from one region to another.

monitor: A device used to record a process; to watch or keep track of.

moratorium: A temporary suspension or delay in action.

mortality: Frequency in number of deaths.

ovulate: To produce or discharge eggs.

periodic: Having repeated cycles.

pigmentation: Coloring in cells and tissues of animals.

poach: To trespass on another's property in order to take game illegally.

quarantine: A period of time during which one suspected of carrying a contagious disease is detained in isolation.

regenerate: To form or create anew.

specimen: A sample of plant or animal taken as a representative of an entire set.

synchronous: Occurring at the same time.

vegetarian: One whose diet consists of grains, plants, and plant products and who eats no meat.

zoologist: A person who studies the biological science of animals.

Suggestions for Further Reading

Caroline Arnold, *Panda*. New York: Morrow Jr. Books, 1992.

Jin Xuqi and Markus Kappeler, *The Great Panda*. New York: G. P. Putnam's Sons, 1986.

Dorcas MacClintock, *Red Pandas*. New York: Charles Scribner's Sons, 1988.

Miriam Schlein, *Jane Goodall's Animal World: Pandas*. New York: Atheneum, 1989.

——, *Project Panda Watch*. New York: Atheneum, 1984.

Tang Xiyang, *Living Treasures*. New York: Bantam Books, 1987.

Works Consulted

Erika Brady, "First U.S. Panda, Shanghaied in China, Stirred up a Ruckus," *Smithsonian*, December 1983.

Louise Branson, "Poaching the Pandas," *World Press Review*, March 1989.

L. Erik Bratt, "Zoo Paves Way for a New Bout of Pandamania," *San Diego Union-Tribune*, January 25, 1993.

Marcus W. Brauchli, "Panda Habitat Gets New Hotel For Eco-Tourist," *Wall Street Journal*, March 8, 1994.

Jeanne F. Brooks, "China Presses Its Bid to Save Pandas," *San Diego Union-Tribune*, September 22, 1996.

———, "Giving Nature a Nudge, for Pandas' Sake," *San Diego Union-Tribune*, November 3, 1996.

Chris Catton, *Pandas*. New York: Facts On File, 1990.

Patricia Dibsie, "Bai Yun, the Girl, to Shi Shi, the Guy: Same Time Next Year?" *San Diego Union-Tribune*, April 30, 1997.

———, "Pandas Please Public, Keepers / Scientists Alert to Chance for Offspring," *San Diego Union-Tribune*, January 15, 1997.

Edward Dolnick, "Panda Paradox," *Discover*, September 1989.

Pat Flynn, "Zoo's 2 Pandas Pronounced in Good Health/Team of 18 Medical Experts Examines Pair," *San Diego Union-Tribune*, October 10, 1996.

Helen M. Fox, ed. and trans., *Abbe David's Diary*. Cambridge, MA: Harvard University Press, 1949.

John W. Grandy, "Plus and Minuses Are Seen in Zoo's Panda-Loan Program," *San Diego Union-Tribune*, January 25, 1995.

Ruth Harkness, *The Lady and the Panda.* New York: Carrick and Evans, 1938.

Karen Kucher, "China Delays Arrival of Pandas at Zoo, but Studies Go Forward," *San Diego Union-Tribune*, December 4, 1995.

———, "A New Era for Policy on Pandas / China, U.S. Zoos to Focus on Breeding," *San Diego Union-Tribune*, April 19, 1993.

———, "Wildlife Group Battles Loan of 2 Pandas to Zoo," *San Diego Union-Tribune*, June 8, 1993.

———, "Zoo Is Denied Permission to Borrow, Breed Pandas," *San Diego Union-Tribune*, September 22, 1993.

Don Lessem, "The Secret World of Pandas," *Boston Globe Magazine*, December 9, 1990.

Los Angeles Daily News, "1st Test-Tube Pandas Expected in 5 Years," March 16, 1996.

Lü Zhi, "Newborn Panda in the Wild," *National Geographic*, February 1993.

Neil Morgan, "Can the Feds Gear up to Save a Panda's Life?" *San Diego Union-Tribune*, September 2, 1993.

National Zoo, "Giant Panda / ZOO / Creating the Nation's First BioPark," August 1996.

Stephen J. O'Brien, "The Ancestry of the Giant Panda," *Scientific American*, November 1987.

Lori Oliwenstein, "What's Black and White and Fading Fast?" *Discover*, January 1988.

Pan Wenshi, "New Hope for China's Giant Pandas," *National Geographic*, February 1995.

Tony Perry, "Biology, Politics Pose Huge Barriers to Saving Pandas," *Los Angeles Times*, June 21, 1994.

———, "Panda Express Hits San Diego at Last," *Los Angeles Times*, September 11, 1996.

———, "San Diego's Giant Pandas Begin a Delicate Courtship," *Los Angeles Times*, March 2, 1997.

Theodore Roosevelt and Kermit Roosevelt, *Trailing the Giant Panda.* New York: Charles Scribner's Sons, 1929.

Ileane Rudolph, "In Pursuit of Pandas," *TV Guide*, March 25, 1995.

San Diego Union-Tribune, "The Late Panda Ling-Ling May Yet Have Offspring," January 1, 1993.

San Diego Union-Tribune, "Panda Fei Fei Dies in Tokyo," December 15, 1994.

San Diego Union-Tribune, "The Panda Paradox / Refusal to Import Shun Shun May Prove Deadly," October 24, 1993.

San Diego Union-Tribune, "Preserve the Pandas / A New Federal Policy Will Foster Survival," December 22, 1993.

San Diego Union-Tribune, "U.S. Moves to Lift Ban on Pandas / Proposed Rules Aim to Ensure Protection," March 31, 1995.

George B. Schaller, *The Giant Pandas of Wolong*. Chicago: University of Chicago Press, 1985.

———, *The Last Panda*. Chicago: University of Chicago Press, 1993.

Pat Shipman, "Killer Bamboo," *Discover*, February 1990.

Walter A. Taylor, "As Rare Pandas Lumber Toward Extinction—," *U.S. News & World Report*, July 2, 1984.

Time, "Battling a Bamboo Crisis," November 28, 1983.

S. Lynne Walker, "BORN to be WILD / A Zoo Is Dramatically Redesigned, and Both Animals and Visitors Are Thrilled at the Result," *San Diego Union-Tribune*, November 22, 1994.

John Bonnett Wexo, "Giant Pandas," *Zoobooks*, August 1986.

Zhou Meiyue, "IVF Project Stirs Debate over How to Preserve Pandas," *Science*, June 14, 1996.

Index

94

About the Author

Wonder at animals, from the firefly to the whale, has shaped the writing career of Judith Janda Presnall. Whether the topic is animals' bioluminescence, skeleton, specialized training, or endangerment, Presnall has craved more knowledge about their existence. Her published books include *Animals That Glow*, awarded Outstanding Science Book for Children by the National Science Teachers Association–Children's Book Council; *Animal Skeletons*; *Circuses*; *The Importance of Rachel Carson*; and *Artificial Organs*.

Presnall grew up in Milwaukee, Wisconsin, and earned a bachelor of education degree from the University of Wisconsin, Whitewater. After teaching high school and college classes for many years, Presnall now is a full-time writer. Both the Society of Children's Book Writers and Illustrators and the California Writers' Club have recognized Presnall for her nonfiction writing. In 1997, she was honored with the Jack London Award for meritorious service by the California Writers' Club, San Fernando Valley Branch. She and her husband, Lance, live in southern California. They have a daughter, Kaye, and a son, Kory.

Picture Credits